How to Get What You Want
in Life with the Money
You Already Have

How to Get What You Want in Life with the Money You Already Have

Carol Keeffe

Little, Brown and Company

Boston   New York   Toronto   London

Library of Congress Cataloging-in-Publication Data
Keeffe, Carol.
    How to get what you want in life with the money
you already have / Carol Keeffe.—1st ed.
        p.   cm.
    ISBN 0-316-48518-7
    1. Finance, Personal.   I. Title.
HG179.K438   1995
332.024—dc20   94-21356

10   9   8   7   6   5   4   3

HAD

Published simultaneously in Canada by
Little, Brown & Company (Canada) Limited

Printed in the United States of America

I dedicate this book to my sons,
Dominic and Mario,
who consistently call me to be my best. I salute
the dreamer, seeker, friend, writer, inventor,
athlete, playmate, creator, and genius in each of
you. May you always choose to listen to your
own voice and have the courage to follow the
path it calls you to.

Contents

CONTENTS

Acknowledgments

I'D LIKE to thank my dad, Mike Keeffe, for his lifelong loving model of authenticity and simplicity. Thank you, Dad, for the profound respect you have shown me all my life, for always believing in me and for loving me just the way I am. To my mom, Jean Taylor Keeffe, I want to say thank you for being a powerful model of generosity. You have taught me there is always room for more at the dinner table and that there is plenty of love to accommodate one more for the night (creatures included). Your beautiful example has shown me how to open my heart to all living things.

Thanks to Gia, whose love and spirit are alive in me, providing me with the security and strength to dare to be myself.

I am deeply grateful to the following people, who, by loving me unconditionally, invite me to believe in myself and be myself: LesLee Reilly Vetorino for always seeing me at the heart of myself; Catherine Dean (Lamerson) Colter for celebrating my beauty and helping to keep life a marvelous party; Carol Brownell Ames for loving and affirming me just the way I am; Chuck Custer for treating me with awe and deep respect; Donna Varnau for believing in me and for continuously inviting me to grow; Gail Carlson for her love, contagious spirit, and beautiful soul; Nancy Keeffe Horyza for her courage to heal and her celebration of me; Nancyanna Dill for being the precious person she is; Mary Ann O'Mara for trusting in me and believing in me no matter what.

I give my thanks and love to the following people for helping me along my path. Each of you in your own unique way has touched my life, and because of your love I am a better person: Connie Durbin, Cindy Poppelwell Schweitzer, John Robert Smith, Jr., Katherine Keeffe Johnson, Dan Jordan, Jean (Eugenia) Keeffe, Marcia Johnson Kelly, Carolyn Traub, Donnie Keeffe, Art Hartley, Sandy Wilson, Tony Hansen, Marcus Erickson, Tom Kelly, Mark Mayberry, Dorothy Craig, Linida Schaffer, Candace Gilmore, Vicki Long, Jerry Magelssen, Mike Dobb, Diana Fairbanks, Mary Harris-Giles, Donna Mae Nunn, Charlene Woodward, Virgle and Beulah Harrell, Karen Bjorback, Murray Gordon, Patty Blunt Hargrove, Rowena Bethards, Dana Becket, Tom Guzzardo, Brian E. Davis, Jeannie Adams Sitter, Herb Bridge, Nancy Mueller, Rosarii Metzger, Delney Hilen.

A special thanks to those who specifically helped me with the book. First I'd like to thank author Susan Page, who, having never even met me, cheered, supported, and believed in me and my book and introduced me to Dorothy Wall (editor extraordinaire) and to Patti Brietman (the best literary agent in the world). A heartfelt thanks to Chuck Custer for his support. Thank you for helping edit my book proposal and for affirming my ability to write. To my agent, Patti Brietman, I owe deeply felt thanks for continuous support, encouragement, guidance, and first-rate representation. My thanks to Janet Abbott for her friendship and invaluable suggestions for organization.

Many thanks to my mother, Jean Keeffe, for her endless

hours of copyediting and particularly for catching glitches and suggesting just the right word or phrase that was needed. Special thanks to Betty Power, senior copyeditor at Little, Brown, for tweaking the copy and for letting me know she liked what I've written. To LesLee Reilly Vetorino for reading and editing into the wee hours of the morning so we could fly off to Hawaii. To Brian E. Davis for reading the manuscript and especially for his uplifting pictures and comments. To Janice Leah Tolnay of Oceana Word Processing for her superb job of transcribing. And particular thanks go to my editors at Little, Brown: Tracy Brown, Mary South, and Jennifer Josephy. I thank each of you for your support, expert help, and belief in me and my work. Thank you to Jen Stein and Abby Wilentz for your warmth, encouragement, and help throughout the publishing process.

A special thanks to the members of NSA (National Speakers Association) — particularly members of the Pacific Northwest Chapter of NSA — for their inspiration and continued support. I would like to express my gratitude to the Associated Students of the University of Washington (A.S.U.W.) Experimental College for the privilege of presenting my paycheck workshop every quarter for the past ten years.

My hat is off to the incredible men and women who have attended my workshops since 1982. Thank you for your questions, participation, and willingness to be vulnerable. I send a huge, warm thanks to each of you who has called, written, or allowed me to interview you. By sharing your struggles, successes, and experiences you are an inspiration to others and have added interest, flavor, and credibility to the book. I am grateful to each of you.

I salute LesLee and Dean and Carol, three gutsy, phenomenal women who light up my life with their love, laughter, and nonstop belief in me. You are my constant inspiration and support. You each see me as I am and love me for being myself. Your belief in me carries me through my toughest times, your love invites me to be myself, and your support encourages me to hold fast to my dreams. I love you Dean, Carol, and LesLee.

Introduction

NO MATTER how much money I ever earned — I spent it all.

When I was young and single — I spent all my money. When I was married with two incomes, no children and a ninety-five-dollar-a-month rent payment — my husband and I spent all our money. If I made more money, I spent more money. No matter how much money there was, it was never enough.

As the years went by, the bills began to mount. Soon the bills felt overwhelming. My goal in life became to get the bills paid off. I kept saying, "As soon as the bills are paid, *then* I'll start to save. As soon as the bills are paid, *then* I'll take the kids to Disneyland. As soon as the bills are paid, then . . . then . . . then . . . Meanwhile, the bills mounted, my anxiety grew, and life was on hold.

Finally I realized that as long as I'm alive there will be laundry to do, dishes to wash, and bills to pay. I faced the fact that my serious put-off-my-dreams-until-later approach was not working — and I began turning my relationship with money around.

I'm not a finance expert, a business major, or a licensed

anything in the area of money. I'm an ordinary person with an ordinary paycheck who discovered money methods that work. I've gone from feeling hopeless and discouraged to realizing I have choices with my money. I went from aimless frittering and believing adventure was only for others (who I thought had more money than I had) to focusing on dreams and making them happen.

This book is about values and choices. Yours. It's about how to embrace what means the most to you in life. I'll show you easy, powerful money-managing methods so you'll be able to do what you love more of the time, and bills won't have the grip on you they once had.

The fact that you have picked up this book is significant — it shows that you have taken control. Money is perhaps the most intimidating and formidable element in our lives. Your choice to read and learn proves you have the desire and courage to make your hard-to-come-by money work for you.

This book is about putting *fun* back into your life — now — with the money you already have. It's a tool to crank up the quality of your life. You'll learn how to eliminate your installment bills painlessly and how to put more satisfaction, excitement, and adventure into your life.

This money approach works because it's easy, fun, and doable. Whether you live on $6,000, $60,000 or $600,000 a year, this book will help. *You* are in charge here. You won't be told what to do; you'll be asked, "What is it you want?" Then *you* will choose — based on what you value most in life.

People have said, "I arrived at your money seminar kicking and screaming." You, too, might be resistant and skeptical, wondering why this money advice should be any different from all the rest. You've learned that most money advice doesn't help. In fact, it's often discouraging, leaving you feeling hopeless. With this method you won't kick and scream anymore. You'll be excited because it's easy to do, it works, and you'll see results immediately.

Kate said, "The main thing I feel is empowerment. I feel like money doesn't have control over me any longer. I decide how I spend my money. It's hard-earned money and I want to spend it wisely. Now we have money for fun stuff! You know we never thought we'd have money for fun stuff." Over and over people tell me this is what they've been looking for all their lives. They've attended financial seminars, read books, and nothing's helped — until this.

"Several years ago my CPA firm attempted to get into the personal financial planning field, and we failed miserably in our attempt," said Tim, a certified public accountant. "What we failed to realize was that the vast majority of our clients did not need financial planning; they needed to take this workshop. How can people worry about investment planning if they (1) have no cash, (2) spend everything they earn, (3) owe a substantial amount of money on credit/installment loan bills. Without the background and perspective gained by attending this workshop, most people have no choice but to wander through life from paycheck to paycheck. I now realize how contrary and radically different the theme of this workshop is from contemporary financial thinking. How refreshing to witness a simple, basic approach to a potential life-changing experience. I hope you can continue converting people to realize that if it is simple and understandable, that's good. So many people think that in order to be good it has to be complex."

Tim's right. You won't find intimidating financial jargon or guilt-causing lists of what you "should" be doing with your money. The guilt trips, shoulds, and oughts have been thrown out. You won't trudge through budget plans and mind-boggling formulas. Instead, you'll enjoy money games to help you reach your dreams.

These ideas didn't just pop up overnight. They're not ideas that *might* work. They're tried, proven, and *guaranteed* to work. Thousands who have taken my seminars since 1982 can testify to that. Today they experience the deeply satisfying feeling of being in control of their money and their lives. Bills no longer consume their attention and their energy. The bill nightmare is over. Kate goes on to say, "We're in big debt, like twenty thousand dollars, so psychologically what helps is that we have several savings accounts each designated for different things. We just went on a short vacation and paid for it with cash! We were really proud of ourselves. We didn't charge at all — not one thing. Wow, this is really different. We can really live on the money we earn and still pay our bills!"

With these ideas, you'll find your energy shifting to what *really matters* to you in life. You'll learn to give yourself permission to reach for your goals and enjoy them when they arrive. Teresa writes, "In the three years since taking your money workshop, my husband and I have had two children, gone from two incomes to one, and have saved $12,375! We're not only managing on one income, we're saving to reach our next goal!"

About now you might be thinking, "I know exactly what's coming next: "Get your bills paid off quickly, quit eating out so much, and save ten percent of what you make." No. You don't want to be told what to do, and besides, that old approach to money is depressing, absolutely no fun — and, frankly, does not work.

What you'll learn is a simple, doable approach to money that puts you in control. The result? You'll feel relaxed and confident. You'll have the know-how to get what you've always wanted. Best of all, you'll be motivated. You'll be chomping at the bit to go for it.

It's your money. You are in the driver's seat. You'll find you have countless choices with your life and with your money. Cheryl writes, "The energy I've derived from this money approach extends to exercise habits, parenting, and work accomplishments. Ideas are opening up. Money is less of a specter and more a tool with which to shape my life. I feel more confident, more assertive, and more active. I can express who I am and what I want in a more complete fashion."

Without realizing it, most of us have been settling for little moments of happiness instead of experiencing the deep inner satisfaction that comes with living for what really matters to us. As you read, you'll begin to believe that you deserve to reach your goals. You'll believe it's not only okay, it's good to spend some of your own hard-earned money on what brings you a deep sense of satisfaction. You'll find your whole life changing for the better — *all with the money you already have.*

How to Get What You Want in Life with the Money You Already Have

ONE

I Don't Have Any Money,
So What Good Is
This Book?

Hold fast to dreams
For when dreams go
Life is a barren field
Frozen with snow.
— Langston Hughes

"Well, this week is payday for both of us. For three days we'll feel rich and then it's gone!"
— *Flight attendant married to a driver for UPS*

"I feel as if I never have enough. At tax time my husband and I figured our income. We were astounded at the amount we made. It was way over what we thought. We sat back and wondered, 'Where did it all go?'"
— *C.P.A. married to an engineer*

"I feel out of control with money. However much I make, I spend too much but never have the sense that I am spending a lot. It seems to escape through the cracks. I'm in debt and would like to get out of debt and have a clean slate. I'd like to save for things I want, like traveling and moving to a bigger apartment. Right now it's hard to imagine having enough money to do the basic things in life, such as have children, live in a house, have a garden, and so on. These things that seem within reach of many people seem like impossible dreams to me."
— *Artist working as a customer service representative at an art supply company*

"I'm tired of being in debt and living from paycheck to paycheck. With only fifteen more working years, I'm concerned about retirement income (or lack of it). I have very little savings and no investments."

— *Loan department supervisor*

"I feel like I never have enough money for all that I want. I would love to be able to spend more. I'm very cautious for the most part but feel sometimes that I'm in trouble, say, if my car has a problem. I also owe quite a bit on two major credit cards. It bothers me how long it could take me to pay them off."

— *Customer service representative*

ALTHOUGH each of these stories is unique, there's also a recurring theme — a feeling of powerlessness about money. Regardless of our income we seem to have the following in common:

- ✦ Spending more than we have
- ✦ Little or no money in savings
- ✦ Installment bills (we try to get rid of them, but they keep coming back)
- ✦ A feeling of helplessness in the face of our bills
- ✦ No "master" long-range money plan

When I finally faced my own pattern, I realized the solution was not more money; it was learning how to manage the money I had.

After working with several thousand people, I've identified a pattern:

✦ We tend to fritter money away in our attempt to bring some little bits of fun into our lives. (Since we feel there's no money for "big stuff," we indulge in the simple pleasures of espresso, magazines, movies, eating out.)

✦ We put little or no money in savings.

✦ We become victims of the bills. Our attitude is, "Poor me, I'll always be trying to make ends meet."

✦ We focus on our bills and become dedicated to paying them off. When eliminating bills is our goal, dreams and fun go by the wayside.

✦ Unconsciously, our thinking becomes, "Happiness equals having the bills paid off." We haven't asked ourselves, "What will really make me happy?"

It's no wonder life has lost its zing. Each month we put as much money as possible toward the bills. Some people even take on an extra job or work overtime — just to reduce or eliminate bills. In the effort to control the bill monster, we lose the quality of our lives. Life is whittled down to two events — work and bills.

Bringing zest back into your life is what this book is all about. The fact that you're reading this says you want to be in control of your life — that you want more peace, more satisfaction, and more dreams coming true. I've learned over the years that anyone who comes to my money seminar is a step ahead of the rest. Whether your money situation is satisfying or frustrating, your choice to learn more says it all.

As you read, you'll hear my own money stories and the stories of others to illustrate how to have the best of both worlds — fun today and tomorrow. You'll learn how to be in control of your money and how to change your circumstances for the better. You'll get both the inspiration and the tools to turn your money situation right side up — now, with the money you already have.

As you read and try some of the ideas in this book, you're going to learn how to order up just what you want in life. You've heard it said, "People don't plan to fail — they fail to plan." Here you'll make your own money plan based on what you love and value most. It will be your custom plan.

In the following story you'll get a glimpse of why most of us haven't been able to figure out a money plan that works.

Marcus came to me because he felt trapped. "I have close to ten thousand dollars' worth of credit card debt and earn thirty thousand a year. How can I possibly pay off my debt and go back to school?" he wondered.

When I asked him how his bills affected his day-to-day life, he said, "It feels like a solid black tunnel with no light at the end. Just the thought of the bills makes me feel tense and overworked."

Reluctantly he told me that a fellow employee had described him as "a cold and driven man" and that the words had cut deeply. Sadly, he admitted, they were true.

He explained that he had gone to the doctor because he was gaining weight and was afraid of high blood pressure (at 29!) and his arms were breaking out in a rash. The doctor assured him that the problem was stress and asked him what he would like to do if he could do anything in the world.

(Smart doctor!) Marcus answered, "To work as a nurse or physician's assistant in third world countries."

I was surprised at Marcus's clarity. Most people have never asked themselves, "What do I want in life?" I asked him to imagine what it would be like if he had a solid foundation of money. He smiled, relaxed, and said, "It would be like sitting in a meadow of wildflowers beside a pond on a beautiful day. I'd feel at peace." He went on to share his desire to have a piano and his longing to travel to Russia.

Given his clear desires, I was surprised at what happened when we started to talk about an action plan. "Well," Marcus said in a lifeless tone, "I know that I'm going to have to give up some things I really enjoy, like expensive coffee and lunches out, so I can pay off the bills." As soon as I mentioned creating a plan, his mind focused on eliminating his bills. He figured he'd have to start depriving himself; his enthusiasm about his goals vanished.

Through Marcus, I got a glimpse of how our minds work. I saw how quickly we switch from the excitement of our dreams and goals to the stern parental-type message to "clean up your room" or in this case "pay off the installment bills." The self-defeating cycle goes like this: We hate bills, so we try like crazy to get rid of them. The goal becomes paying off the bills. The result of that kind of goal? We work harder and longer hours in order to make more money. This creates more tension, more stress, and more need for "expensive coffee and lunches out" to buy some inner peace and relaxation.

In response to Marcus's assumption that he would have to deprive himself of the simple pleasures of life, I picked up a piece of paper and tore it into six pieces. I labeled one

INSTALLMENT BILLS; others were RENT, FOOD, CLOTHES, MISCELLANE-OUS (gasoline, toothpaste, batteries . . .), and GOALS (piano, travel, and nursing school). I placed the piece labeled "INSTALL-MENT BILLS" down first, then followed with RENT, and so on, with GOALS in last place.

INSTALLMENT BILLS

RENT

FOOD

CLOTHES

MISCELLANEOUS

GOALS

We looked at this priority list and talked about what it feels like to get up in the morning, day after day, with the purpose of life being to "pay off the bills." Marcus was looking somber.

Then I took the last piece of paper, GOALS (piano, travel, nursing school), and put it at the top of the priority list. I placed the INSTALLMENT BILLS at the bottom — leaving the normal life expenses in the middle.

GOALS

RENT

FOOD

CLOTHES

MISCELLANEOUS

INSTALLMENT BILLS

Marcus leaned forward. "I can't believe it! I never would have done this, but it's starting to make sense." He mentioned that he had been thinking of taking on a part-time job (in addition to his twelve-hour shifts at his computer night job) but that his friends had really discouraged him. Then his face lit up. "I've got it! Before, I was going to take on more work and more stress in order to make bigger payments on my installment bills — still never putting anything toward what I really want."

The chances are that if Marcus had taken an extra job, his bills would have increased — not decreased. With more work and longer hours the body's need for rest, relaxation, and sanity would escalate. He'd spend more money "buying" inner peace through food, clothes, alcohol. Not only would tension fill even more of his life, but his dreams, the things that are the heart and soul of inner happiness, would have been even farther than ever from becoming real.

It's the trap most of us fall into — we've put life on hold while we wait and hope that our finances will improve. I was impressed with Marcus. Here he was at age twenty-nine, putting his life together already. If you are quite a bit older than Marcus and are just now taking hold of your money dilemma, I know it can be painful. It's difficult to look back on all the years of doing without, putting off, and waiting — just to find out we're pretty much where we were when we started!

It reminds me of the woman who wanted to become an attorney but said, "I can't because I'm already forty-five years old and it will be seven years of school and study before I can even take the bar exam." Her friend's wise response was, "How old will you be in seven years if you *don't* study and become an attorney?"

It's time for us to take a new look at things. The question we must ask ourselves is, "What brings me joy? When do I experience that wonderful feeling of satisfaction? What is it I really want in life?"

For too long we've put off living — waiting until things settle down, until the hard times are over, until the bills are paid. Recently I heard of a young man living out of his car. One day while talking about his passion for music, he was offered the use of a piano. Within a week he had a part-time job, had hired a piano teacher, and had begun saving for his own keyboard. What happened? He had become motivated.

Most people in his situation would never consider following their heart's dream. The guilt and pressure from parents, friends, and society would overwhelm them. "You can't live in your car! It's disgraceful. Go get a job and a decent place to live." That would be the beginning and the end of the message and the focus.

I'm not suggesting that we be irresponsible. I am suggesting that we look at what we've been conditioned to think and do. The message from "out there" is clear: "Get your life in order first and then (if the day ever comes) search your heart for your dreams." We can learn from this young man living out of his car. When he became motivated, his life began instantly to turn around. He had a reason to get up, a reason to find a job, a reason to go to work. He grabbed hold of life and took off, his passion for music leading the way.

In a workshop one evening we had a chance to go into this in depth. Jeanette volunteered that she felt certain she was born to compose and play music. Her goal was to own a piano keyboard so she could begin composing again. She explained she works at a job she dislikes and owes thousands on her installment bills. "I just seem to drag through life feeling over-whelmed and drained."

As I continued teaching, asking the group to focus more keenly on what they really wanted in life, Jeanette became frustrated and demanded, "How can I even consider my goal of buying a keyboard when I owe so much money? My parents and friends will accuse me of being irresponsible. I feel guilty just thinking about having a keyboard."

I asked the rest of the group if they could identify with what Jeanette was experiencing. Heads nodded affirmatively throughout the room. Then I asked, "What do you think Jea-nette's relatives and friends would do if she started saving for a keyboard? What would happen if they saw her enjoying life as well as paying her bills?" "They'd get angry," someone said. "They'd become jealous that she is reaching her dreams and they aren't," commented someone else. "They want to be in control of her, so they'd come on even stronger, pushing re-sponsibility — trying to make her feel guilty for wanting a pi-ano keyboard when she's in debt."

Thanks to Jeanette's sharing, the message that most of us got growing up became clear. Work first and then play. Com-pany can't come over until the house is cleaned. No fun until the bills are paid.

We haven't been raised to prioritize and make decisions based on our own values about money. Many people in my workshops have said, "But my problem is that I play too much. I enjoy eating out and buying little luxuries, but when it's time to pay the bills there's never enough." Whether we're making bills top priority and putting off life until they're gone or whether we're blithely ignoring financial responsibilities while we "live it up," the results are the same. We lack the inner satisfaction of being in control of our money, and we don't experience the deeper inner happiness that accompanies achieving what we really want in life.

What can help us to let go of our old patterns that aren't working? What can help us zero in on what we really want in life? The answer: to become motivated.

What would happen if you were given tickets to an event or a place you'd love to go? — a concert by your favorite singer, the Academy Awards, or a trip to a dreamed-of vacation spot? If you had tickets in hand, you'd be motivated! You'd work harder and faster and do everything you could to make it to the event.

You'd suddenly have energy you didn't have before you got the tickets. Now you're not just thinking and talking about the event — you're going. If all this excitement and efficiency would occur when someone dropped tickets in your hands, just imagine what would happen if *you* planned and got tickets yourself?

Getting the tickets yourself means finding out what you love about life and choosing to go for it. It means starting to live now — whether the bills are all paid and all of life feels under control or not.

Allow your mind to wander aimlessly over all the things you love to do. Daydream about the activities, people, places, and pastimes that bring you satisfaction. Keep this dream door open over the next few days and weeks and jot down every thought that comes to mind. Think back to when you were a child and the times you were the happiest. Capture the particulars — exactly what was it that made those times so special?

What are the places you planned to see by now? What are some of the things you've wanted to have and do?

What we're doing is shifting our energy and our focus from the dead-end path where we put life on hold to the satisfying open road where we experience purpose in life *today*.

You might be grumbling, "You don't understand! You don't have the bills I have. You don't have the handicap . . . the monstrous cost of living . . . the stresses." It's true. I don't know your individual circumstances. You must have plenty of obstacles — even some that seem insurmountable. Probably all of us have said, "I'll get started when things settle down" or, "I'll begin when things get back to normal." Meanwhile, life passes us by.

HAVING FUN WITH YOUR MONEY

Let's get started right now with the easiest and most popular of all the money games. The ¢hange Game — the game that changes your life while you save your ¢hange.

Most of us have saved our change at some point in our lives — perhaps on top of the dresser. And most of us have just about the same amount of change now that we had years ago when we started putting it there.

This time we'll be doing a lot more than just casually tossing change on a dresser. Begin by focusing on one specific goal. Think of big things (like a new sofa or a trip to Australia) and small (a new wallet or an overnight in a getaway not far from home). Think about short-term fun *and* far-off goals. Maybe you want a new winter coat or the chance to go out to a nice relaxed dinner more often. Or maybe what comes to mind is the trip you've longed for all your life. Carolyn got motivated to begin saving her change because she wanted a scratching post for her cat (or, really, wanted to preserve her furniture). Take a few minutes to visualize some of the things you want to see, do, and have.

Now, while you're thinking of all the things you like, take the change in your pocket or purse and put it on a surface in front of you. (When you actually take the change in your hand for your goal, you've started the momentum. You're not thinking or wondering — you're doing.) Keep asking yourself what you want your first goal to be. Something small and immediate? Or something bigger and a bit farther down the line? The size or cost of your dream doesn't matter. What matters is that you want to make this happen for yourself.

This is not the time to help make someone else's dream come true. If you'd like, you can do that in addition to your own goal, but for *you* to get the boost from this money game, *you* must feel the success. An attempt to make someone else happy too often backfires. We accidentally set both of us up. The other person may look at what we did and be disappointed in the color, size, or timing of our gift. They may be angry because they wanted to achieve the goal themselves rather than have it handed to them. The only way to guarantee success is to do this for yourself. So choose a goal that you really want; then you're guaranteed to feel satisfied when you get it.

Also, you may want to keep your goal and stash of change a secret. Others may criticize or poke fun at what you're doing, trying to rob you of your enthusiasm and hope. People may say the ¢hange Game is "childish." Childish? No. Child*like?* Yes. The truth is, kids are masters at making boring jobs *fun.*

And that's exactly why the ¢hange Game works — because it's so much fun.

The next step is to take the change you've collected from pockets, dresser, or purse and place it in a container (a mug, glass, jar, plastic container, peanut can). Now for the critical step: on a piece of paper, print exactly what you are saving your change for, and tape this paper on your container. The reason the ¢hange Game works so dramatically is that you've *written down* your goal and posted it on your change container. The label is as important in the ¢hange Game as a key is to starting a car. With your container clearly labeled Hawaii or Evening on the Town you are focused on what you really want and are motivated to go for it. (I created the Dream Box to help get people started. It's a practical, environmentally friendly container designed specifically for playing the ¢hange Game.)

The trick at first is to give yourself permission to want what you want. What happens for so many of us is that within moments of feeling the rush of excitement over our goal, we realize our partner, friends, or relatives will criticize what we've chosen. We imagine them questioning or poking fun at our goal and we freeze. As we consider the likelihood of others giving us the third degree, we pause, step back, and most of the time abandon our idea. It doesn't seem worth the criticism and discouragement we'll get from others.

Someone always seems to question and discourage our actions no matter what we do. So we might as well choose something we really want. Most of my life I spent waiting in eager anticipation for others to notice me, approve of me, and give me the gifts of time, attention, and things that I wanted — but disappointment was what I usually got. I had given away control over my own life and its outcome. No more. Now *I* decide and take action on what's best for me.

Next, with permission to give yourself something you really want, *go for it.* Grab a container, label it with your goal, and start dropping in all the change you can gather.

In the past you may have taken pride in dipping into your pockets and making the exact change at the cash register. Well, now the pride comes from keeping all the change you see and putting it toward your goal. Before you know it you'll figure out all kinds of ways to collect more change for your goal. For example, instead of writing a check at the grocery store for the exact amount, you'll round it up to the next dollar so the checker will give you change.

No matter how bleak your money situation, there's always change to be found. The most frequent comment I get is, "I love the ¢hange Game because it's so painless. I don't even miss the money and I love reaching my goals." Hawaii, Europe, mountain bike, sofa, dance lessons, dinner out, romantic weekends away, Caribbean cruise . . . are a few of the dreams that have come true for people because of the ¢hange Game.

Anne talked on the phone with me one day about her change. "I used to buy a lot of things that I became bored with or never used or didn't need because I had that spur-of-the-moment 'I've-just-got-to-have-this' feeling. Well, now I've learned to put money aside. I have this jar, I'm looking at it right now, this really huge jar, that when I come home I put, you know, spare change in it and extra quarters and all that kind of thing and every once in a while I have a real blast and just go out and decide to waste it all. But I have learned to put money aside for the long term, the short term, and the merely frivolous."

How to succeed at the ¢hange Game:

1. Name a specific goal that really motivates you.
2. Label your Dream Box with your goal.
3. Save all your change until you reach your goal.
4. Enjoy your guilt-free dream come true!

I encourage you to give yourself the boost and satisfaction *now* instead of waiting until you've finished this book. Start today to make your money work for you. You know what you want. You won't be disappointed, because you're in charge of making certain you succeed.

So, grab any container you can find, label the container with your goal, and drop in all the change you can find. Unless you label your container, two things are guaranteed to happen: (1) the money will disappear for this and that, and (2) without a fun vacation or item you're eagerly looking forward to, there's no reason to save your change. Labeling your Dream Box is the crucial step.

Right now you may be energized and thinking to yourself, "Gosh! This is a great idea. I'm going to save my change for season tickets." But still nothing has happened. Your challenge is to move past lip service and beyond awareness into action: to label the container with a goal that really motivates you and every day drop in all the change you can find.

If you can't decide between a trip to Hawaii and a new computer, then toss a coin and choose one. Get started. Too often we lose all momentum before we've even begun because we don't decide on a goal. Remember, you can always change your mind. If you decide you'd much rather relax on the warm, sunny beaches of Hawaii than upgrade your computer — simply relabel your container. What's important is that you'll already have money saved. A written goal gives us a *reason* to save our money and builds in the excitement and motivation to take us all the way.

With your container labeled, you're ready to play the ¢hange Game. For the next seven days save *all* your change. If you're at the store and an item costs $4.69, pay with $5.00 (or a check for $5.00). The cashier will give you 31¢ in change. When you arrive home, take all your change from the day and plunk it triumphantly in your labeled container. You have chosen to make your dream come true. And you can see it happening.

You may be thinking, "Whoop-de-do! I need twelve hundred dollars for my dream vacation, and you're asking me to drop my pennies in a jar. Give me a break." But, you know, it really does work. I suppose it's like standing at the bottom of a mountain and hearing someone tell us that the way to get to the top is to put one foot in front of the other. It works.

So many people have called to tell me about their vacations to Hawaii, Mexico, the Caribbean . . . all on the change they've saved. Sandy called and listed the items she and her husband purchased in just the first year of playing the ¢hange Game: motorcycle equipment, a telephoto lens for their 35mm camera, china, and living room furniture. One gentleman congratulated his son and new daughter-in-law with a check for $1,500 on their wedding day. He had saved his change from the time of their engagement to the wedding, fourteen months later.

Over and over again people say one of the greatest things

about saving their change is that they don't feel guilty cashing in on their goal. That's what the money is set aside for.

Each time you find a quarter or a cashier gives you change, you'll get pumped. You've built in healthful daily shots of adrenaline. Each dime, penny, or quarter means you're that much closer to your labeled goal. There's no mystery, no investment counselors, no complex graphs. All you do is grab your change each day and put it in your labeled container each night. Soon you'll have the final result. It's simple. It's easy. It works.

Watch out, though. Too often, just as we're eager to start a new activity, our mind starts to question and find fault with it. Before we know it, our head has come up with an endless list of reasons why the idea won't work. Our excitement's gone and we've lost again. Not this time. Start *today* before the idea can be destroyed by your logical mind. This isn't left-brain, logical stuff, this is fun stuff. Go for it. Your momentum will carry you all the way to your goal. Will you give yourself permission to go for your goals?

A practical suggestion: Every few weeks pour all your change on the kitchen table along with some paper coin rolls. (Just ask for paper coin rolls next time you're at your credit union or bank. They're free.) Before you know it you (or your family) will be sitting around the table rolling the money, adding it up, and feeling energized. Some banks will roll your money for a small fee, but you probably want to enjoy the satisfaction of counting your own dream money and keeping the fee money for yourself.

Many people find it motivating to place a picture of their goal on their ¢hange Game container. Vanna clipped and pasted pictures of rings from jewelry ads to decorate her box. She commented, "Seeing the rings and having my Dream Box out as a reminder helped me realize how long I've wanted a ring and helped me get it much faster." (Until then, Vanna had been waiting for her husband to buy her the ring.) Henriette cut out a small photograph of herself, placed it on a postcard of the Eiffel Tower, and taped it on the front of her daily planner. Each time she saw the picture, she was reminded of what she really wanted. She stayed focused and motivated all the way to France.

Don't wait for the perfect jar. Don't wait for the perfect goal. Start.

What day is today? If three days from now you haven't labeled and started your jar, you probably never will. Do yourself and everyone you know a favor — act now on your dreams. There's no question about it. When we're happy and fulfilled, we're much nicer to be around. Everyone wins. Most of all *you*.

You may be feeling a bit skeptical and resistant. Perhaps you're saying to yourself, "I bought this book because it's supposed to be a radical new approach to money management. I've been told my life with money will be transformed, and so far I've been told to dream about all the things I want in life and put loose change in a box."

Starting out this way probably does seem naive. One reason we have trouble with this approach is that most of us learned at an early age not to ask for what we want. As kids we were *told* what to do and what was good for us. "Get out the door right now!" "Make your bed." "Clean your room." "Eat this, it's good for you." "Sit up straight." "Of course you'll like it." Many of us were not encouraged to have a mind of our own. As adults, to some degree we continue to do what we are told. We buy the brands, drive the cars, and work at the jobs our parents, teachers, and the media tell us we should.

With this money approach, *you* are in charge. The heart and soul of this method is not in this book. It's in you. Inside these pages are merely ideas, tools, and stories. It is you who will change your life by embracing your hopes and dreams. It's knowing what you really want in life and choosing it for yourself that will fill you with passion and drive, thus transforming your life.

What are your dreams? What do you love about life? Keep searching. Find out what makes you tick.

Lois wrote, "I'm a forty-three-year-old single parent of two teenage boys. I took your money class because I felt lost and frustrated with no goals or future plans and was going deeper in debt. Extra money always went to pay bills and buy food and clothes for the boys. I now have fun goals such as a new stereo, a cruise to the Bahamas, and a condo with a view — as well as a retirement fund and an emergency fund. My teenagers are saving, too — for a stereo and a TV."

One woman said she listened to me on the radio one day. "I just kept thinking how ridiculous your comments sounded. Then, as the week went on, I realized how much sense it all made!"

I watch this happen in my workshops. As I introduce the first ideas, people listen politely, skeptically, even hopefully, but not really believing this money seminar is any different from all the others. As we round the corner into the third hour of class, their eyes brighten. Their energy level is up. Smiles on their faces reveal hope and relief. They can see that their money situation *is* manageable and surmountable. They're thrilled to know that there *is* a path to their hopes and dreams, and best of all, the way is fun and easy.

When I ask people who have attended my workshop, "What was the key element for you in getting control of your money?" again and again they say, "Before your class, I had never really thought about what I wanted."

The reason most things don't happen is that our mind-set doesn't even allow the possibility. "It's impossible in my situation" or, "We can't even consider it until the bills are under control" or, "We can't afford it." We throw out ideas before they even have a chance.

Our challenge is to ask the vital new question, "How important is this to me? Is it what I really want?" Entertain all ideas and let them simmer inside. The simmer test always works. If the idea comes from your heart and fits into the grander scheme of what has meaning for you, then the idea will grow and blossom and keep tugging at your heartstrings. As the idea simmers inside of you, you'll know, because if it's something you really want, it will bring a smile to your face and a zip to your step.

DO I HAVE A CHOICE?

Most of us don't have choices. Why? Because we don't know we have choices. We've been operating from the outside in — taking our cues from the shoulds and oughts of the world rather than going inside ourselves for direction. We feel we have to go to work, have to go to school, had better say yes, and must do things a certain way. Often what we thought was a choice or our decision was really just going along with some-one else's rule or agenda for us. Too often we forget to go within ourselves to find out what we really want. We forget to ask ourselves seriously, "What is the best and wisest choice I can make based on my values and what I want for the final result?"

What would your first response be if you were asked, "How many choices do you have when the alarm goes off?" One time in a workshop someone blurted out, "Two!" So, for that person there are only two choices. Actually, each moment of the day we have countless choices. When the alarm goes off, we can stretch and roll over, turn the alarm off, and go back to sleep or we can push the snooze once, twice . . . a dozen times. When the alarm rings, we can get angry or we can celebrate and embrace the beauty of life and all the opportunities the day holds. When the sound awakens us, we can slowly drag ourselves from the bed or we can bound out, dancing into the new day. How many choices are there for us each moment? One? None? Or are they countless? The answer is: We only have as many options as we can recognize. Until we realize we have countless choices every minute of the day, our lives can't begin to be transformed.

It's critical to realize that even within the limits of our particular situation, we still have innumerable choices. To see how many we have means shifting from living from the outside in (living by rules and shoulds and the agenda others have for us) to living from the inside out (listening to what has meaning and importance to us).

This may take time. Most of my life I didn't have a clue how to listen to myself and figure out what I valued. Responsibilities of work and family dominated my life. My inner voice was drowned out. Occasionally a good movie or photograph in a magazine would stir my hidden dreams, but the demands of life soon swept those thoughts away. The idea of listening to yourself may be new and uncomfortable or even scary. That's okay. Acknowledge those feelings and go easy on yourself. For now, just crack the door and take a peek to see what your innermost thoughts and feelings are. There's no hurry. Each peek is another step, and each step takes us closer to choosing the fullness and joy in life we all deserve.

At the end of the money workshop, Amy wrote, "I like and am aware of the word 'choices' — what a fun word! I am excited about saving and getting my goals. I'm no longer a prisoner. I'm no longer ignoring financial matters. If anyone is going to solve my money problems, it's going to be me."

A tip: Next time you are in the throes of making choices, notice how many you come up with. For example, your car is in for repair and you need to find a way to get to work for the next two days. Immediately you realize you have two alternatives: you could ask a coworker for a ride or you could take public transportation to work. You begin to decide what to do.

When you find yourself at the point where you're starting actually to make your next decision, stop. Pause to challenge and really s-t-r-e-t-c-h yourself. Come up with at least two other viable choices.

For example, how about renting a car or, cheaper yet, renting a used car or calling a cab? Perhaps this could be your opportunity to call the carpool phone number you've always noticed on the freeway, or a chance to meet other people in your neighborhood.

By looking beyond your first and obvious options for even more choices, you are tapping into your creative mind. As you leave the familiar and wander into the unknown, the ideas become less conventional and often much more appealing and fun. You might decide that, since the car is in the shop, it's an opportunity to take a day off just to relax at home (after all, you won't be tempted to run a bunch of errands). Granted, you may not choose the option of taking the day off or of calling about carpools. But by allowing yourself to entertain as many choices as you can possibly think of, you have greater freedom and are more in charge of your life.

What goes on in your mind? Ask yourself throughout each day, "What *other* choices do I have right this moment? Am I doing this because I want to or because I think I should? If I feel I must do what I am doing, is there another, more palatable or more rewarding way I could approach this?"

With choice comes power. But first we must know we have a choice. Jot the word CHOICE in big letters on several different pieces of paper and tack them up on the mirror, at your work space, on the refrigerator, and on the car dash-board. Seeing the word CHOICE throughout the day will help remind you to keep e-x-p-a-n-d-i-n-g the options you have. Listen carefully to the wise voice from within that knows what you value most — that part of you that knows what will bring you the greatest satisfaction in the long run.

Here is the simple yet profound three-step progression that will take you from where you are to where you want to be.

Values	(Step 1)	DISCOVERING what *really* matters to you
Choice	(Step 2)	CHOOSING based on what you *value*
ACTION	(Step 3)	ACTING according to your *choices*

Three easy steps, so difficult to carry out. Too often we never even make it to Step 3.

Step 1, Values, is finding out what you care most about

in life, realizing just which activities, people, and places bring you happiness and the feeling that you're glad to be alive.

Step 2, Choice, is learning to make the small and large decisions of life *based* on what you value. This step is often tough. Even when you know what you value most, choosing it may be difficult. For one thing you may feel guilty or obligated to meet the needs of family or to please others instead. You may have to begin slowly and allow yourself merely to "think" about choosing what's important to you.

Here's the progression so far:

VALUES ➤ CHOICE

So far so good. We are choosing based on what we value. The problem? Most of us never get past step 2. I remember one of my first experiences in trying to let go of my workaholic behavior. What happened was that I actually considered the thought of how good a relaxing long bath would feel instead of a quick shower. It made sense that if I'd take even fifteen minutes to get away from all the demands on my time to just soothe and relax my body, when I emerged I'd be a renewed and much more patient mother and person. I knew what I valued (a relaxed, refreshed me), and I consciously chose, "I'm going to treat myself to a soothing bath."

The problem? Nothing happened. Two years went by and I still hadn't taken a relaxing bath. Steps 1 and 2 were important because my awareness was heightened. Being in touch with what I wanted, and choosing what I valued would help me to be my best self. But the fact is, I hadn't taken the bath! Steps 1 and 2 were critical steps, but without step 3, nothing had really changed.

VALUES ➤ CHOICE | **_DEAD END!_**

Nothing happens until we ACT. Until I actually ran the water, escaped my busy life, and climbed into the tub, nothing had changed.

VALUES ➤ CHOICE ➤ **_ACTION!_**

It may be new to focus on yourself and what you love to do. You may even feel guilty at first, afraid of all the feelings that stir inside as you begin to think of what would bring you satisfaction. You may be afraid that your new choices will upset others. Many people will want you to stay the same, particularly if you've given up your own dreams in the attempt to make others happy. (I put my own life on hold for eighteen years trying to make someone else happy.) The one person we'll always be with is ourself. Our ultimate commitment in life must be to our own self — because it is only when we have taken exquisite care of ourselves that we are our very best. And why would we want to be our best? So we can bring that very best to others — our partners, children, friends, clients, patients, coworkers. Just imagine if we each made the choice to take care of ourself first — imagine the warmth, the presence, the patience, and the positive energy we would each bring to others and to life itself.

Why do we admire Abe Lincoln? Because he was himself — real, honest, down-to-earth. Why has Walt Disney had such a profound impact? Because he focused on, believed in, and acted on his dreams. And Mother Teresa? She has found deep inner happiness wanting to work with the poor — and choosing to do it. All of these people became aware of what they valued most in life and then acted.

The fact is, bills and hardships are a given in life. They're guaranteed. But happiness? It's not a given. It's a choice. It's time to stop waiting for happiness and start choosing it — now. When we stop and think about it, usually our happiest days are the ones when we have something to look forward to, the days we're going cross-country skiing in the morning or we're meeting someone special for dinner after work. When we're planning and doing what we *love*, we're energized, productive, and motivated.

The goal? To thrust you into action and into choosing to make your life full and complete now, with the money you already have. Your job? To open the door to your dreams and keep it open. Life will always throw obstacles your way. The trick is to stay focused on what you love — the precious people, activities, and places that make your heart soar!

TWO

Pay Yourself First

The future belongs to those who believe in the
beauty of their dreams.
— Eleanor Roosevelt

Dear Carol,

When I took your money management class, I had zero in savings or investments and my credit cards were fairly high. In three years I have truly made a change in how I manage my money. I *do* pay myself first! Today I have over $8,000 in investments and $6,000 in my savings, which I plan to diversify! I also, as you recommended, changed banks and found a VISA account with 12% interest and no yearly fee.

I said I always wanted to travel . . . well, I spent over three weeks touring Europe with some of the money I had saved.

I should mention that I do not have a high income (less than $25,000/yr) nor do I share my living expenses with anyone. It sounds like the last three years have been rosy. They have not. I have had to move four times and have gone through great emotional turmoil in my personal life. At times I felt my world was crumbling around me, but I think knowing that at least this one area of my life (finances) was stable gave me reassurance. It also made me feel good about what I had accomplished and the positive changes I had made.

Anyway, I just wanted you to know that your class and all the energy, information, and enthusiasm helped point me in the right direction. You certainly helped to make a difference in my life.

I hope all is going well with you. Thank you and keep up the good work!

> Sincerely,
> Vicki

W HOA!" you say. "How'd she do it? The answer is in her words, "I *do* pay myself first!"

"But wait a minute." You balk. "If I pay myself first, there won't be enough money for the bills." Or maybe you're saying, "Since there already is not enough money for the bills, how can I possibly pay myself at all — much less first?"

Most of us know we "should" be putting money in savings, that we "should" be saving for vacations instead of traveling by credit card or loan (or even worse, staying home!). We realize we "should" be socking money away for a rainy day, retirement, kids' college. So we admit we "should," and most of us even say we "will" pay ourselves as soon as . . . the bills are paid, as soon as . . . we get a raise, as soon as . . . we change our job, as soon as. . . . Meanwhile, life is going by while we wait. We're continually putting off our dreams and goals, the very things that give each day meaning and purpose.

When I say, "Pay yourself first" in a workshop, people don't seem to react at all. I could have said "Exercise regularly" or, "Floss daily." They've heard it so many times before that they begin to tune out instantly. They sit unaffected, waiting for me to get on to something new. Well, I don't move on. I stay on the subject of taking money off the top — for yourself. After a few minutes people begin to get pretty irritated. If I were to remove the politeness from their statements and add the inflection they're feeling, it might sound like this: "Look, we're over ten thousand dollars in debt and we've got two kids who will soon be in college. We can't possibly pay ourselves first. We want something that will help us get out of the trap we're in, not pipe dreams. How can we possibly pay ourselves first *and* save money for our dreams when we owe so much and make so little?"

Diane doesn't pay herself first. She writes, "My greatest concern is the future. I am very obsessive about paying bills and tend to pay over the required amount, which makes me short on funds when the end of the pay period rolls around. I work two jobs — both good paying — and cannot seem to save any money." Noni writes, "I was so hoping that my finances would permit me to attend your upcoming seminar. But money must go to my priorities of bills first."

What about *your* bills? How important have they been in your life? Take a moment to explore the feelings you experience when you think about your bills. What words describe how you've felt toward your bills over the years? In a workshop people readily shout out their feelings, and we quickly come up with a list pretty much like this:

FEELINGS ABOUT BILLS
Frustration
Anger
Resentment
Relief (*very* temporary)
Stress
Hopelessness
Depression
Overwhelmed

Anxiety
Endless

At this point, with the column of feelings about the bills filled, I ask people to get in touch with the energy they've put into achieving their goals. Again, I ask them to call out the words that describe those feelings.

The room falls silent.

After a moment of the silence, Shirley, sitting with her husband (both are retired), said, "Gee, my goal has always been to pay off the bills!" Shirley actually said what most of us have lived.

Note the contrast from people jumping in their seats to shout out how it feels to try to pay off the bills — to mouths dropping open and bodies falling back into their chairs in silence when asked how much energy they've spent reaching for their goals. In effect, all energy has gone to the bills, nothing into making dreams and goals come true. (Even if some of us have spent energy striving to reach our goals, it's usually a mere shot in the dark compared to the tremendous amount of effort, energy, and struggle that we've expended attempting to conquer our bills.)

If we stopped a hundred people on the street and asked each one, "What is your goal in life? What are your fondest dreams and deepest aspirations?" people might say, "To be a movie star. Own a ranch in Montana. See my children grow up happy and healthy. Live to enjoy my grandchildren." Surely no one would answer, "My one and only goal in life is to pay off all my bills!"

Here's what the picture looks like for most of us.

ENERGY EXPENDED ON OUR BILLS	ENERGY EXPENDED ON OUR GOALS
Frustration	
Anger	
Resentment	
Relief (*very* temporary)	
Stress	
Hopelessness	
Depression	
Overwhelmed	
Anxiety	
Endless	

Pause for a moment and *feel* the difference as you read the full left column and the empty one on the right. Feel how the negative emotions around the bills have drained your life energy. The tension, stress, and anxiety of the bills have created such clamor in our lives that they drown out our dreams. Our goals sit in silence, unnoticed.

It's time to shift our focus off the bills. It's time to recognize that our hard-to-come-by money is *ours* and that it's our dreams and goals that give life meaning. Lynn said, "Before, I didn't want to spend my time at work. Now, I'm happy to work. The more I work, the better, because the more goals I'll be able to have. Now I'd work overtime if I could because that would be more money for my goals." It's time to recognize that the money we earn is *ours* and start directing some of it toward our dreams as well as toward our bills.

Jeanette spoke up at this point in one workshop. "But what about the bills I've incurred? *I* made the decision to buy those things or charge my meals so it really is *their* check."

Jeanette expressed what most of the group was feeling. "*My* paycheck? I don't think so."

Jeanette said what so many of us feel. "Yes, of course these bills are mine." But when we're asked to claim our paycheck — the money we've earned by getting up each morning and putting in hours and hours at work — we resist. "My paycheck? Couldn't be. This belongs to the bills."

Jeanette's resistance helped me see more clearly than ever the grip the bills have on us. My mind was racing for some way to drive the point home, to help people in the workshop grasp this new concept. I felt like shouting, "This is the money *you* worked for, the check is written in *your* name. It's *your* money!"

I asked people to hold out both hands. "Imagine you are holding your bills in one hand and your check in the other. They both bear your name. Which do you claim as yours?" As I held my hands out — bills in one, paycheck in the other, I watched people's faces. I could tell they wanted to believe that this was their check. But they couldn't. Only one hand went out, the one holding the bills.

Here's a fascinating human pattern. Even though focusing all our attention on getting rid of the bills is overwhelming and depressing, it's familiar. And the fact is, we find comfort in the familiar. Stepping away from what we know is uncomfortable, even frightening. So, unless we're highly motivated or thrown against our will into something new, we usually stay with what we know. We may peek out and long for what we want, for what might be, but we don't venture out into the unknown.

Turning the key in your front door opens the way to the comforts of your home. Paying yourself first (even *one dollar* from your paycheck taken off the top for you) cracks the door to a new life for yourself.

By taking one dollar off the top of the paycheck and giving it to yourself, you are saying, "I am important. I have worked hard for this money, and I will reward myself (and those I love) by securing some of it for me (us)."

Why don't we pay ourselves first? Because, before the check even arrives, we know the money is gone to the bills. By the time we pay the rent/mortgage, light, heat, credit cards . . . , there's nothing left. "The paycheck isn't ours," we say. "It really belongs to the bills."

Let's look more closely. Yep. The check is addressed to you. So before you start writing checks to everyone else, pause and remember who earned the money. *You did.* "Before, when I would list my bills, I never had savings on the list," remarked Mary Ann. "Or if I had it on the list, it was on the very bottom, and it was the thing I crossed out when I ran out of money. Now it's at the top of the list. Because if I don't pay me, no one else will. That's for certain." She's right. *You* earned it. You deserve to earmark some of the money for you before you begin doling it out to the phone company, VISA, the electric company, the department stores, the heat company. Think about it. You earned the money. Not only do you deserve some of the money you earned, you need some to cover the expenses of day-to-day life.

Choosing to pay ourselves first is difficult for most of us, and sometimes it seems nearly impossible. Carol, a thirty-three-year-old mother and legal assistant wrote, "I feel guilty paying me. I know what you said, and I understand the theory. And I agree. However, I still feel guilty saving for me when I owe money to Sears or MasterCard, etc. I'm going to try your approach . . . but I still feel guilty. I keep hearing my mother's voice."

Her mention of her "mother's voice" is significant. Our conditioning early in life continues to affect us today. Here's what happens for me when I revisit that time. When I close my eyes, I can begin to remember myself at a young age. Sights and sounds come into focus. I see my sisters, my house, and me. Then suddenly I hear, "CAROL! Wait your turn! Do what you're told! Don't make a fuss. Think of others first. Work first and then play. Settle down. Be careful!"

How did those messages affect me? Early on I learned that the "right" thing was to put others first, not to think of myself, and not to feel what I was feeling. "Carol, all you ever do is think of yourself." I pull back as I remember hearing those words. Is that all little-girl Carol ever did — think of herself?

As a child those words hurt me deeply. The message I got was, "Other people and other people's things are more important than I am." I became keenly aware of the feelings of others. I must care for others and their property above all. I learned to keep my focus outside myself, on others. Accused of being selfish, I was motivated all the more to prove that I was not selfish, that I was generous and giving. By the time I was an adult and on my own, almost my entire focus was on others. I was constantly proving myself.

No wonder I was so confused as a child. I tried to make sense of a statement that wasn't true ("All you ever do is think of yourself"). Now, with perspective, I can see that the adults were exaggerating to make a point. They were unaware of the damage they were doing. Those words left me hurt and confused about myself. Although my memories don't deal with money, they do deal with a basic attitude. I entered adulthood

focused in two misdirected ways: (1) listening to others because they knew better than I did what was best for me, and
(2) taking care of others first.

When I look back at how I interpreted life when I was
little, I understand my adult behavior better. With no new information to alter those messages, I stepped out into the adult
world feeling less valuable than others. I would knock myself
out trying to prove that I was important and worthwhile. I'd
take my paycheck and faithfully pay others first, trying to
demonstrate that I was not selfish, that indeed I was taking
care of others first. I was constantly trying to prove those
childhood messages wrong. "I am responsible. I'm caring,
hard-working, and reliable." I'd pay all I possibly could out of
the paycheck toward the bills and then, with what was left,
my family would limp through the month, using credit cards
when the money was gone.

One evening in the money seminar Lisa spoke up, explaining that her problem was the opposite of mine. She said
she was the youngest of six and was spoiled from day one.
Her older brothers and sisters waited on her and bought her
everything her heart desired. "Here I am, an adult," she said,
"and I expect to get everything I want. So what do I do?
Charge everything."

In my case, I continued my childhood behavior by running up big bills trying to take care of others and prove I was
worthy. Lisa ran up big bills trying to continue to shower herself with everything she wanted as she had become accustomed to doing as a child. Neither one of us was making decisions based on *what we valued or what was best for us.*

In order to change the way we handle money today, as
adults, it's helpful to understand what messages we picked up

as a child. One of the biggest messages for a great number of us was that we weren't important — that a clean house, polite manners, and the feelings of others counted a great deal — but not us. A good place to start in rewriting those childhood messages is to begin *choosing to feel important.*

One day I started thinking about six-year-old children. I imagined them sleeping, exploring, running, and laughing. I realized that every single six-year-old in the world is precious and lovable. Then I saw myself at six and realized that I must have been special and lovable, too. The point? Since we're not likely to pay someone we don't like, a first step for many of us in learning to pay ourselves first is learning to like ourselves and to accept that we are important.

Each of us has our own history and learned coping mechanisms that affect our relationship with money today. What's important is that we be honest with ourselves. Willpower (unfortunately) doesn't work in matters that are deep-seated — at least not for long. In order to really change, we each must acknowledge the patterns we learned as children and begin to let them go. With the "shoulds" and "oughts" disappearing, we can begin to listen to our own inner voice. We can begin to give ourselves permission to listen to our own heart and choose happiness for ourselves.

Here's an experience I had that was significant in helping me shift my energy from others to myself. I had made an appointment with a financial adviser in hopes of getting some control of our family's money situation. I remember standing beside her as she thumbed through the financial papers I had brought. After a minute or two she handed them back to me, and said, "Is this it?" Sheepishly, I nodded my head. She gave me a what-are-you-wasting-my-time-for look and ushered me out the door, saying, "Come back when you've paid off your bills."

I walked out of her office and over to the elevator feeling embarrassed and humiliated and with the words ringing in my ears, "Come back when you've paid off your bills." As the elevator doors closed, something clicked in my head. "Wait a minute! As long as I'm alive, I'll always have bills. For ten years I tried desperately to get rid of our bills, and all that's happened is that we have more bills now than ever."

That did it. I stepped off the elevator a different person. Month after month, year after year, I had put life on hold, saying, "As soon as the bills are paid off, *then* I will start to save, *then* I'll begin to do all those things I love to do." Because of the financial adviser's look and words, I got upset enough to see things in a new light. I had a new reality. There will always, always, be bills.

Finally, I was seeing bills (installment bills in particular) for what they really are, one of the dozens of responsibilities in my life. I realized that bills are no different from dishes that need doing or laundry that needs washing. Finally, the bills took their proper place in my life — one of the many, many responsibilities I deal with — but certainly NOT an overpowering, all-consuming responsibility. Every day until my last I'll be brushing my teeth, getting dressed, cleaning up, paying the bills, eating, talking. Ahhhh, finally I had perspective. As long as I am alive I will generate bills. (Heck, I'll even generate a few after I die!)

The all-consuming black cloud that the VISA, Sears, and other department store bills had formed all those years vanished. For the first time I had the "big picture" of life in front of me. I wasn't willing to wait for the installment bills to be paid off to start to live. I was deciding to make the choice to start living now!

I feel lucky that I had an "aha" experience. For me everything came together that day. For you, however, coming to the understanding and determination to have the installment bills take a less-important role in your life may take some time and a great deal of convincing. Your challenge? To put bills in the back seat and your dreams up front with you.

Unconsciously, many of us live as if someone or something else is going to take care of everything for us. Let's take a closer look. What can (or can't) we count on? How about a pension? Pension money is usually either tied up with the company or is invested. If the company goes belly-up or the stock market crashes, so goes our retirement money. How about social security? Can we feel secure in counting on social security money being there for us when we need it or being enough if we do receive it? How about an inheritance? That's another emotion-packed money source that we had better not count on. And the lottery? On the average in the U.S. the chance of winning a jackpot is one in 4.5 million. So what is left that we can count on? Ourselves. What a difference it made in my life when I quit being anxious about whether there'd be enough pension or social security and started *doing* something about it myself.

I finally started to get a perspective on money. For most of my life fifty dollars was a lot, five hundred was a huge chunk, and five thousand dollars was, well, sure to be spent in no time at all. During the time in my life that the pendulum was swinging from out of control (or others in control) to the realization that it is *my* life and *I'll* begin choosing what's best for me — I saw large sums of money in a new way.

At one point I wondered what I'd need if my income stopped and I had to rely on myself. I imagined I had socked away $200,000. At first this seemed like a huge amount of money, but then I realized that if I was used to living on $30,000 a year, I'd deplete my savings in only seven years. Then I refigured, planning not to touch the lump sum of $200,000 but, instead, to live on the interest generated by the money. If I were able to get a 10% return on my money (easy some years, not even possible others), that would be 10% × $200,000 = $20,000. This way, year after year, I would receive $20,000 in interest payments while never depleting the total lump sum.

These calculations gave me a whole new perspective on the question "How much is a lot of money?" Suddenly $600 or $3,000 was no longer an amount to burn a hole in my pocket. Now that I wanted control over my life and my future, I knew that $200,000 was a *minimum* amount to save for myself. An income of $20,000 for an entire year is not all that much — especially down the line.

Making the decision to pay ourselves first is tough. My friend Tom struggled with the idea of paying himself first for over two years. He took my money workshop and came by for a private session; money was a frequent topic of conversation. Though Tom is open-minded and could clearly see how paying himself first made sense, it just wasn't clicking for him.

Then one day he called. "Carol," he said, "I've finally got it. I'm going to India. I'm through saying I want to go. I'm going. I want to leave in about eighteen months, and I'm hoping to take my sixteen-year-old daughter with me." Tom finally put together what money management is all about: *finding out what you want in life* and going for it.

If Tom follows through and actually travels to India, he will have given himself the taste of success with money. The daydreaming, wishing, and wondering will have been transformed into — "I did it!" With success comes confidence. "I did it before, I can do it again." I didn't come up with the idea of putting $200,000 away for myself right away. At first it would have been incomprehensible. But as savings grew and big family vacations came to be, I gained confidence in myself and my ability to affect my own financial situation. Since loose change could mount up to a thousand dollars in a year, I began to believe that a few dollars from the paycheck each month in a retirement account would build to create a secure future. Ahhhhhh. I liked what was happening. My choices were paying bigger and bigger dividends.

∾

It seems that most of us settle for brief moments of happiness — the kind that comes with a candy bar, magazine, or latest kitchen gadget. Unconsciously we operate from the position that we'll never be able to do all we want. So to soothe and appease ourselves, we fritter money away.

How much might slip through *your* fingers in one day? Let's see . . . a Coke here, an espresso there, perhaps a quarter in a video machine, or maybe a new tape or CD. Let's say $3 a day escapes on nonessentials (pop, cookies, coffee, magazines, jewelry, you name it). You may be saying, "Hey! I don't spend a dime all week. I catch the bus every day, take a sack lunch, and come straight home every night, never spending beyond the bus fare, which is an essential." Okay. Now it's your day off. Is it possible that you find yourself in a store and end up buying a shirt or blouse regularly priced at $59, marked down to only $21? Or maybe you go to the movies with a friend, buy some popcorn, and go out afterward for a midnight snack — spending all together about $21.

Let's see, $21 ÷ 7 days in the week = $3 a day. So even though you didn't spend any money all week, by spending $21 on the seventh day you averaged $3 a day. So let's use $3 as an amount that might slip through any of our fingers on a given day.

When we multiply 365 days in the year times $3 (average spent on nonessentials), it becomes $1,095!

$$\begin{array}{r} 365 \\ \times\ \$3 \\ \hline \$1,095 \end{array}$$ per year!

It's hard to believe. We so often settle for fleeting moments of joy, when by sneaking away just $3 a day, we could have over a thousand dollars for the things we really value in life. Check out the following formula:

Poor me = frittering money away

Have you ever noticed that when you're feeling sorry for yourself, you're more likely to spend money in order to help you feel better? For years I felt sorry for myself because we were four people trying to make it on one salary. It always seemed that everyone else had money for fancy vacations and beautiful furniture, but we had to just scrape by. To soothe the pain of "never having enough" we'd all go out for ice cream or head for the movies.

Realizing that $3 a day equals over $1,000 a year was a major discovery for me. One thousand dollars. ONE THOUSAND DOLLARS! That figure kept shining like a neon light before me. I would pick up a clever little item at the store and look at the price, $3.29. Yikes! This isn't just $3.29. This could be one thousand dollars!

Let's say you're at the grocery checkout stand and you see a magazine with several articles you find interesting. Without thinking, you toss it in with your groceries to read later at home. Suddenly your mind clicks in. "What am I doing! Just $3 a day becomes over a thousand dollars in a year. Put that back!" You respond to your critical voice by dutifully replacing the magazine, and you continue on through the cashier's line. As you leave the store, you notice all the other people with their magazines, candy, and cookies and you say, "Poor me. It's not fair. Everyone else gets to buy fun little things, but not me."

Or you can shift to a new mode of thinking. "I'm so glad I stopped myself from buying that magazine. When I give it some thought, it's not what I really want. Right now I'll take the money that I would have spent for the magazine, and I'll put it in my pocket. When I get home, I'm taking that three twenty-four and dropping it in my Dream Box." You're walking taller and breathing deeper as you celebrate your choice. "That's over three more dollars for my _____. I'm arriving at my goal faster than I ever dreamed I would!"

ॐ

What else keeps us from paying ourselves first when the paycheck arrives? One reason we don't succeed at saving is that it's b-o-r-i-n-g . . . zzzzzzzzzzz. Holly wrote, "My one savings account never had any money in it because I never had a label on it. It never had a name. It never meant that much to me. Just money to be spent."

What makes the difference? Saving *for something.* Holly continued, "Now I am thinking about what I really want to do (take a trip to Alabama to visit Lucy and drive to New Orleans for the Jazz Festival. How fun!). It has a name. I also have an emergency fund for the emergencies that are always coming up. Now I won't take the money out of my Alabama trip if something comes up."

What a difference! Good-bye boredom. Hello goals! Saving for something you love works. It's motivating, inspiring, and fun. Whether it's a trip, a new computer, a better job, or the choice to work only three days a week — what you really want is exciting and life-giving. It will get you jumping out of bed in the morning, and you'll *want* to save for it.

In my conversation with Anne she went on to say how her thinking has changed. "I'm a lot healthier now. I'm getting what I really want in life and learning to make the choices. I think a lot of times in the old days I'd buy things because I thought I ought to. I wouldn't have anything to do, so I'd go shopping, that kind of thing. I realize now that a lot of things I was buying and taking home never made it out of the package because I didn't really want them. I realized that while money doesn't buy happiness, it can buy material things and comfort that contribute to it. When I started to make choices about what is it that I *really* want and when I make the plan to save the money — it's satisfying when I get it because it really does mean something to me. Every birthday I give myself something extravagant. It always costs a whole lot of money and I'm really happy."

ALL OR NOTHING

What's another reason a lot of us don't save? Because we operate out of ALL or nothing. As we're paying the bills, we say things like, "*If* there's any money left over, *then* I'll put some in savings." Since there's seldom, if ever, "extra" money after paying the bills, no money makes its way to savings. We tell ourselves, "If I can't put at least fifty or a hundred dollars into savings, then it's not worth putting in any at all."

When's the last time you put $4.19 into savings? Or deposited $1.63 or $14.77? Most of us think that would be ridiculous — a ridiculously small amount of money. So what do we add to our savings? NOTHING!

(By the way, if you did slip away $4.19, $14.77, and $1.63 into an account each *month,* you'd have $249.08 by the end of the year. If you slipped away that much each *week,* you'd be treating yourself to $1,070.68 in a year's time! Just a little here and a little there adds up.)

Have you noticed that we approach a lot of things in life from the extremes of all or nothing? If there's a garage or closet to straighten out, we seldom think of putting away just two or three things. If it's income taxes or an important letter that needs to be tackled, we rarely approach it by setting the timer for fifteen minutes and making headway by fitting it in here and there in our lives. What most of us do is wait and put off until we have a large chunk of time to work on the project; meanwhile, there's no progress at all. Either there's time to get the whole dishwasher loaded or we don't even load one plate.

A twenty-minute walk or none at all. A long letter to a friend or no note at all. When was the last time you paused from a project at home or work for just forty seconds and jotted a note to someone special in your life: "Hi _____, Just wanted you to know you are special to me — hope all is well." You'd feel great sending it. The person would feel wonderful receiving it. Somewhere between all or nothing is a place that pays big dividends when we discover it.

I first recognized this all-or-nothing pattern in my life in regard to putting money into savings. If there wasn't at least $100 dollars "left over" or "extra" in the checkbook after paying the bills, then I didn't put *any* in savings. Not even a dollar.

Most of us don't even consider doing just a little. We say, "But I don't like to do a little; once I start, I like to finish," or "If something is worth doing, it's worth doing right." No wonder so many areas of our lives go neglected.

Our all-or-nothing approach to life keeps us from fun and accomplishment. It loads us with feelings of guilt and pressure for not starting certain projects or for starting and not finishing others. We feel bad if we don't put any money in savings for months and months, and we feel just as bad if we put in a lot at the beginning of the month and then take it out by the end of the month.

It's time to rewrite the old saying, If something is worth doing, it's worth doing right. NO! If something is worth doing, it's worth doing. Period! Just $10 each month slipped out of one paycheck becomes $120 by the end of the year. That's $120 more than you'll have if you don't tuck any away!

Five dollars. What could such a small amount of money do? If, starting from the time you were born, your parents had put just $5 a month (about $1 a week) in the bank for you (earning 5.5% interest) — and if you were forty years old to-day, you would have $8,700. Not bad for a mere $5 a month. But what would have happened if care had been taken to get higher interest during the forty years of saving? If the savings of $5 a month had earned an average of 10% (just 4.5% more) you'd now have $31,800 instead of $8,700. Though the interest rate was not even twice as much more (from 5.5% to 10%) you would have accumulated $23,100 more with the same little five-dollar-a-month deposit — almost four times as much money!

The message? Pay attention to the interest rate. People have told me, "But I like the tellers at my bank," or "My bank is so convenient." Is the convenience or staff worth $23,100 of your money? (I realize rates may be lower than 10% as you read. In the years since I started managing my money, I've seen interest rates range from 16% down to 2.5%. I included this example using 5.5% and 10% to illustrate why we want to get every bit of [safe] interest possible. Once you get your money into savings, *keep track of it*, and make certain you're getting the best interest you can for the present time.)

It works in life, it works with money. A little here and there adds up to lots — doing *something* rather than all or nothing. Anne continued, "You haven't seen me in a long time, but I've lost a hundred pounds. Part of that is I now walk more places instead of taking the bus or my car. I usually try and walk five miles a day. It's not that I don't sit around in the evening eating cookies, I do — it's just that I don't do it seven nights a week anymore. When you go on a diet and all you can have is grapefruit, the day has to come when you can't stand it any longer. You start eating everything in sight. The money I used to spend on bus fare (because I couldn't stand to walk one block) and the money from the junk food I used to eat, I save that now, too. Since I took your course and make choices and decisions about what I really want, I have extra income from the changes in my lifestyle. I get a lot more satisfaction out of money because now I determine what it is I really want and put my money toward it."

Where and how does the all-or-nothing approach operate in *your* life? When do *you* approach a person, place, or thing with the all-or-nothing attitude?

Here's what happened when Donna started thinking something instead of all or nothing. "Money was just something I didn't have and probably wasn't ever going to have. I didn't really worry about it that much, but I also didn't have or aspire to have anything. Now I realize I want a lot of things and I can get them. Once I got the picture of how I could get things by starting small, then I started thinking of big things that I really want to do — like going into business for myself. Now my goal is to have the money to start my business by next year."

A few years ago I was giving a money seminar to a group of Head Start parents. Everyone in the group was living below poverty income level, and most, if not all, were on welfare and food stamps. I'll never forget the young woman sitting off to my left. Shortly into the program she became quite irritated with what I was saying and let it be known that she couldn't possibly "pay herself first" on her income. "There's not even a penny . . . *not a penny* left by the end of the month," she said vehemently. As I was winding up the seminar, she volunteered that $25 would come out first, every month. She spoke with determination and with tears in her eyes. "No matter what happens, I'm taking $25 each month for me and my kids," she declared.

Incredible inner satisfaction comes with our choice to do something rather than all or nothing. How much satisfaction and joy have we passed by because we thought we needed to do something "right"? Here's a saying I read once that has become one of my favorites: "It's more important for me to start to do the right thing than it is to wait until I think I can do it just right."

∾

The reason traditional money seminars haven't helped most of us is that the solution to money management is not so simple. Money issues deal with the gamut of human emotions — guilt, fear, self-pity, insecurity, pride, need for validation, control, and so on. The reason this approach to money *does* work is that it acknowledges our patterns and emotions in relation to money. We're removing the fear and the lectures that tell us what to do. Instead, we're placing ourselves before a smorgasbord and asking — what would taste good? We choose for ourselves what we really want.

Pause for a moment to get a picture for yourself. Either take out a sheet of paper or just close your eyes and pretend a blank sheet is in front of you. Imagine three things taking up space on the page: you, your bills, and your dreams. Take a moment to get a feel for the size, shape, and color of the bills. How about your dreams, goals, and aspirations? Where are they on the page? Where are you in relation to your bills and your dreams? I encourage you to take a few seconds to sketch what you are imagining. What you learn about yourself and your relationship to your bills and goals can be liberating.

In a workshop, Dorothy, a thirty-seven-year-old teacher, drew a stick figure of herself holding out her arms. Her bills were in boxes stacked on her arms, one on top of the other, way above her head. She was surrounded by a black cloud. Her goals were a tiny triangle way off to the side of the page. Dorothy writes about the picture she drew of herself, her bills, and her goals: "My income is shrinking, my bills are growing, and I'm about to fall on my head. My goals are always set aside because I'm too busy just trying to make it to the next paycheck. I feel angry at myself because I think I have wasted so much money on things that brought only temporary happiness. I was raised to believe that money management is denial — you can't have the beautiful things you want."

John, a forty-two-year-old nuclear engineering technician, drew a picture of his goals trapped inside thick walls of bills surrounded by barbed wire. He was a tiny figure off to the left of the trap. John wrote: "It often seems like my goals are surrounded by some really formidable obstacles. I feel insignificant when confronted with the inertia of my situation. The problem is not the generation of money, rather, it's the wise application of funds in day-to-day life."

Pearl, a sixty-year-old business owner, drew herself satisfied to be able to meet her expenses, but her goals were drawn down and out of the picture. She explained, "I pay all the bills for personal and company expenses. The bills aren't overwhelming, but my goals are on the floor, far away from me."

Though the images we each have are different, the experience is predominantly the same — the bills are large, powerful, and looming, and our goals are somewhere out of reach.

Is it any wonder we don't pay ourselves? The good news is that once we're in touch with our own image and obstacles, we can begin to change the picture. We can begin to shift our focus onto our dreams.

People frequently ask me, "How do I decide how much to start paying myself?" The answer? Start giving yourself *something*. Start small. Be realistic. Perhaps you'll begin by placing $3 from each paycheck into a fund for a trip to a favorite vacation spot, and you'll take another $6 to begin an emergency fund.

Be careful. Without realizing it, the skeptic in you may scoff at a mere $3 or $6. It reminds me of how we often tackle an exercise program. We step out the door planning to walk only one mile the first day, planning to build sensibly to a healthful several-miles-a-day routine. But after the first mile we feel so good we continue on for ten and then can't get out of bed the next morning! The end result? We scrap the whole exercise plan and are back where we started. We don't want that to happen with our money!

What's most important in starting to pay ourselves is to start. Do whatever works. Maybe you'll send a check for $8.50 to a relative across the country asking him to promise not to bank it until you've reached your goal. Starting might mean playing the ¢hange Game or taking $6.00 out of every paycheck, stuffing it into a sock, and storing it in a safe place. The approach you take or how much money you put away is not what matters. What's important is that you *start*.

The whole idea of jumping in and starting reminds me of the day I was switching my sons' rooms. About the time that I got their beds and most of the stuff in their rooms out in the hall, I noticed how much Dominic's room needed painting. I stood in the hall as my mind swung from "There's no time to paint his room now" to "Carol, this is the time to paint it — while everything is off the walls." Once I asked myself the pertinent question, I stopped fluctuating. "Do I want the room looking fresh and clean or is it acceptable to me the way it is?" (It hadn't been painted since the house was built some fifteen years previously.) I had my answer. I grabbed some paint from the garage and started on one wall.

It wasn't long before I had to quit. I capped the paint, wrapped the roller, and finished moving and setting up Dominic's bed. What happened next was that every time I'd pass by his bedroom, I'd see the beautiful section of freshly painted wall. It was as if the rest of the room was calling to me, *"Paint me. Paint me."* Up to this point in life my approach to big projects like this was to wait until I had an entire day with nothing to do but paint — precisely the reason Dominic's room hadn't yet been painted.

I found myself grabbing a few minutes here and a couple of hours there. I'd put my son to sleep in my bed and paint for a while in the evening. On the weekend I might snatch another hour or two. Within a month his room had a couple of fresh coats of paint and looked great.

What a lesson for me. My decision to jump in and start painting was a life-changing experience. I discovered that by *starting* I created momentum.

What worked with my son's bedroom walls works with money. START. Take $6 from your paycheck, first, off the top, and put it in a jar, or open a credit union savings account earmarked for something — weekend away, winter coat, new sofa. When you actually take a few dollars in your hand first each month and tuck it away — you've created momentum.

Like the painted wall, it calls to you. After three months you notice there's $18 tucked away and you'll say, "That was sooooooooo easy! I think I'll start taking $11 instead of just $6 out of the paycheck first each month to pay myself."

Before you know it, the jar or the savings account is thriving, and you're putting in more and more money. You'll start opening other accounts for car repair, kitchen remodeling, skis, and the trip you've always dreamed of.

With this approach I'm not going to tell you how much to save because then the driving force becomes guilt. Feeling we must put away a certain amount becomes another obligation, another stress, and another place to fail.

The reason this approach works and works so phenomenally well is that we begin by putting away a small, realistic amount of money for something we're really motivated about. Labeling a container and dropping in our change is such a subtle activity that at first we don't even realize all that is taking place.

So often our attempts to alter our money situation have involved cutting back, getting serious, and doing without. When we abandon those old futile practices, the change in the money part of our lives sneaks up on us. As we effortlessly and painlessly fill our Dream Box, something *is* happening inside. We begin to realize that saving money and getting what we want doesn't have to be a major ordeal. Then, when we see how fast the money is growing, we're motivated to make it grow even faster. And once we've started, the jar or the savings account will call to us, "More money for Europe, please. Christmas is coming; send more $$$$."

Remember, we don't really "save" anything by passing up a purchase. As you reach to buy the coffee, CD, or whatever, the question to ask yourself is "What do I *really* want?" Only you can honestly answer that question. As you give yourself permission to go for your goals, you'll become an expert in seeing the multitude of choices and in carefully weighing them. You'll look at the $3 item you're about to purchase and ask yourself, "Would I rather take the three dollars and put it toward (Europe, the new skis, the kayak . . .), or is this the way I'd like to spend the money right now?" As you do this more and more, you'll discover that sometimes what you really want is the small snack or item. Then there'll be other occasions when what you'll really want is to grab that few dollars *right then* and take them home to your Dream Box.

One of the reasons this approach to money works so well is that we're eliminating the feeling of being deprived. The idea isn't to do without. The idea is to do *with* — what you really want. It's key that you take the money you decided not to spend and make certain it gets home and is placed in your Dream Box.

Remember, if a thing is worth doing, it's worth doing. Period. There will be no gold medals for starting big. Here the winners are the ones who start small and realistically but put forth faithfully, like the tortoise — who won in the end. By tucking away small, realistic amounts of money *each* paycheck, the tortoise easily kept up the pace. Over time the money grew, and the tortoise arrived at his goal!

THREE

Did You Say, Pay the Minimum on My Installment Bills?

The significant problems we face cannot be solved at the same level of thinking we were at when we created them.

— Albert Einstein

D O you want your credit card bills to go away for good? Then pay only the *minimum* payment due each month.

"WHAT? Start paying the *minimum* due on my installment bills?"

"You've got to be kidding!"

"What about the eighteen or twenty-one percent interest I'm paying?"

"The bills will *never* be paid off if I pay only the minimum amount due."

"That's ridiculous and irresponsible."

"I don't like bills. I want my bills paid off quickly."

It's true. Paying only the minimum due on the credit card bills (installment bills) sounds bizarre and irresponsible. Yet often the things that make the least sense at first work best — like the flight attendants' instructions on an airplane. Parents are instructed to put on their own oxygen masks first and then help their children and others. Initially this sounds wrong, as if we were to abandon our helpless children. Then we realize that we'll be useless to our children and others unless we're alive and breathing, and we accept this course of action. So, like the airplane oxygen mask, this idea to pay the minimum on credit card bills sounds wrong initially — until we understand.

Before I go into detail about why and how to pay the minimum, I want to acknowledge that the desire to have our bills paid off is an admirable one. In an ideal situation the solution would be to remove all debt — and have all laundry cleaned and ironed, our cars tuned and washed, our closets and desks organized and clean, and photographs in photograph albums. But life isn't "ideal."

For me, the installment bills always took priority. Every single month, as I sat with the pile of bills, my goal was to get them paid off. I would calculate every angle I could think of, and I always put more money toward the bills than we could afford, in hopes of getting rid of them faster.

I paid as much as I thought I could at the beginning of the month, and at the same time I was putting little or nothing in savings as a backup. (If some money did manage to make it to savings, it was only a matter of time before it was needed and withdrawn.) So when money was gone, out came the credit cards to buy the things we needed to get through until the next payday. And so it went.

Month after month, year after year, I tried desperately to pay off our credit debt. The result? After ten years we had more bills than ever! At first I thought maybe this uncontrollable urge to eliminate bills was my own unique fixation. But I have come to realize that I am not the only one with this over-whelming need-to-pay-the-bills-off syndrome. After over a de-cade of presenting money workshops, I know that almost all of us are hooked — our efforts and energy and money are fun-neled toward one goal — to get the bills paid off and under control.

After all those years of trying the principled approach to getting control of my money, I finally stepped back and admit-ted that not only was my admirable plan not working, it was interfering with the quality and enjoyment of everyday life.

My years of teaching have taught me that the concept of

paying the minimum on the installment bills is an extremely difficult hurdle for most people. And if you're a left-brain, analytical, economist type, it may be quite a challenge for you to accept this approach. Some never do. It's radical. It's fun. And what matters most is that it works. If you follow this approach, not only will your credit card bills be eliminated once and for all, but you will find yourself becoming empowered and in control of your money.

There are basically two kinds of bills: (1) the monthly bills that come with the basic necessities of life like rent/mortgage, electricity, water, garbage, and (2) the bills we accumulate by borrowing the money for the things we can't afford to pay for now (installment loans and credit card bills).

The first category will always be with us because as long as we use water or turn on lights, we'll get a bill to pay for the service. The second category reflects the times we've stretched beyond our means. For whatever reason, we have borrowed from a credit company to allow us to have something today, knowing we'll be paying for it over many tomorrows.

Look at your bill and compare the number stated as the "minimum payment due" to the amount of interest charged on the accumulated balance. The minimum payment should be *more* than the interest accrued. If not, *switch companies!* Recently there have been a few unscrupulous companies whose minimum payment does not reduce the total balance. This is outrageous. Make certain you are not involved with such a company.

Another reason you will want to switch companies is to get the lowest possible interest charges. (My current VISA card charges 5.9% on the unpaid balance.) You can call or stop by your library to get a current list of credit card companies charging the lowest interest on the unpaid balance. Both *Money* magazine and *Kiplinger's Personal Finance* magazine print lists regularly. Remember, credit card companies *want* your business. The new company will make it extremely easy for you. All you need to do is sign the form they will send you and indicate which credit card balances you would like them to assume. Within a couple of weeks you'll receive a bill from the new company with the lower interest rates and statements from your other credit companies that the bill has been paid in full.

Something I heard on the radio one day helped me to feel the effects of my pattern with money. The airlines were having a price war, and round-trip tickets from Seattle to Los Angeles were only $59. Los Angeles meant seeing my grandmother, my uncle and aunt, and, of course, Disneyland. I was acutely aware that if payments hadn't been due on seven credit cards, we could easily have bought tickets for the four of us. We could have hopped a plane Friday after work and school, enjoyed a fun-filled weekend in California, and returned Sunday night — tired and renewed. If we had been living in the present instead of taking today's money to pay for stuff we bought in the past, we could have taken advantage of the California opportunity.

I was finally beginning to recognize my pattern, and I hated what I saw. We were merely existing from paycheck to paycheck, barely getting by, and all the while slipping deeper and deeper into debt. I wanted out of the trap and I wanted money in the bank. Money that was mine (not borrowed from MasterCard, department stores, the bank, relatives, or insurance companies). I was finally beginning to operate from the inside because I had finally asked myself the right question:

"Where do I really want to put my energy?" I realized I didn't want the endless rat race of work, bills, work, bills. What I wanted more than to have the bills gone was to be happy and to enjoy life *now*.

What I really wanted was the freedom of CHOICE. The choice to pursue the classes, travel, and everything else I had put on hold. I wanted the choices that automatically accompany having money.

My realization of what I really wanted was helping me to see what I needed to do next. My goals were motivating me into action. I was determined to figure out a way to save money for what mattered to me.

Once again the key is choice. Obviously what I had been doing for the past ten years was not working, and it was time to make new and different choices. I began checking out finance books from the library and signing up for money and investment workshops.

As I sat in a finance workshop one day, the instructor asked for a volunteer. I raised my hand. "How old are you?" "Thirty-two," I answered. She stretched out a sixty-inch measuring tape, marking the distance from zero to thirty-two with her hands. "Carol," she said, "if you do as well financially in the second half of your life (she stretched her hands from thirty-two to the end of the tape) as you have done this half, how well off will you be?"

Gulp. Stunned and red in the face I got the point. Let's see. If I have $5 in savings at age thirty-two, I'll have $10 in savings at age sixty-four! And if I have $5,000 worth of debt now, I'll be $10,000 in the hole at age sixty-four. Not good.

Seeing where my choices were leading shook me. The truth was that if I couldn't put money away now, then I never would. If I couldn't slip a little into savings while my kids were in diapers and wearing hand-me-downs, then whom was I fooling to think that later, when they were teenagers, saving would be easier! (By the way, my boys *are* in their teens now and our food bill alone is astronomical!) The tape measure experience shook me up and brought me crashing down — to reality. I was shocked, paralyzed — and then grateful. This experience was exactly the jolt I needed to finally take a look at my approach to money and admit, "This does not work."

I'm telling you about my years and years of dedication to paying off the bills and putting no money away to let you know I understand the grip the bills have on us. I want you to know I'm not dishing out theoretical ideas or impossible suggestions. I'm sharing simple, practical ideas that work. It's critical to keep remembering that managing money is not about budgets or percentages. The crux of money management lies deep inside of each of us in what we value. Once we get a strong grip on our passions and dreams, we begin to feel a sense of purpose. When our heart soars at the thought of what we're doing, then we know we're on the right path — we're energized, engaged, and eager to put time and love into whatever it is.

We'll begin getting in control of our situation when we admit that what we've been doing isn't working. I finally admitted it when I heard the cut-rate airline prices. I became determined that the next time opportunity knocked, I'd be ready with cash.

My thinking went, *"If I pay the minimum amount due on my bills, I obviously will have more money in the checkbook. If I have more money in the checkbook, then I'm better equipped to pay cash for what I need instead of using my credit cards. If I have less money going out, then I could sneak some into savings."* My focus was shifting, and the grip the bills had was finally starting to release.

LIVING ON CREDIT KEEPS US LOCKED IN THE PAST

When we make a payment on a credit card bill, we're taking today's money and sending it off to pay for things we bought sometime in the past. And, worse than that, using our credit cards keeps us locked into the urge to pay the card off first and then start to live. So as long as we use credit, we're choosing to put off living.

Let's look at the credit card thinking. (It really is rather strange.) If I don't have the cash to pay for the item today, what causes me to think that my next paycheck will have a superabundance of money — enough to pay present expenses plus money due from the past? For me, the whole credit card trip was a game, and the only person I was fooling was myself.

"Before, I always felt I had to pay twice the minimum payment, and then I'd have no cash," said Mary Ann. "I wondered why I was always broke and why I still owed the same amount. It was a vicious circle. When I started making little minimum payments, it took about two months before I could stop using the card. That was a major change for me. I'm still doing this. I don't feel this panic about paying them off anymore, either. I have plans, and I feel like I'm more in control. I can't believe it. I actually have money in the bank. What a foreign concept!"

Bonnie wrote, "Eight months ago we quit using our credit cards. I have found that not charging purchases on my card has led me to making thoughtful decisions about what I want to spend my hard-earned money on, not just acting impulsively. The result of all the above is that our charge card debt is less. And I don't have this strong guilty conscience that came every time I used a credit card and added to our staggering debt. Spending money is fun now, without guilt."

Before we go any farther, it's important to mention that having a credit card in today's society is convenient and sometimes almost essential. For example, have you ever tried to rent a car without a major credit card? Using your card for actual payment, however, is not usually essential.

Should you carry credit cards? If so, how many? Which ones? Is it okay to use them? Remember, there are no shoulds or oughts. We're going to a new source for the answers to all these questions. We're going to the one person who knows — ourself. The bottom line is for each of us to be totally honest with ourself — finding out what works for us and what doesn't. It doesn't matter what works for someone else; you must find what works for you.

At first, when I was still struggling with the whole credit card problem, I needed to take my cards out of my wallet and leave them at home. (A few good suggestions I've heard over the years are: hiding them in the farthest corner of the attic under the insulation; digging a hole in the backyard about three feet deep and dropping them in; placing them in a bowl of water and freezing it. Then, if you truly needed to get to your credit card to hop a plane to be near someone you love, you could access the card.) Today I could lug around all the credit cards there are because I've made the decision not to use them. I've fallen in love with the freedom and relaxed feeling of control I get from planning ahead and paying as I go.

Only you know what you need to do. Lots of people have

admitted that not having a credit card in their wallet doesn't slow them down at all. They find the perfect tie or blouse and explain to the clerk, "I'm sorry, I don't have my card with me." "No problem, Mr. Smith, we have it here on the computer." So get to know yourself. Do what you need to do to ensure your own success. But first, you need to take the time to find out for yourself what you really want.

Remember, money is an emotional issue. It's loaded. Tony wrote, "When I was feeling depressed, I'd use my cards to make myself feel better. The final result was that I'd feel even worse." Practically every move we make (big or little) is based on how we feel — where we live, what we eat, what clothes we wear, to name a few. And each one of these emotional decisions ends up affecting our pocketbook.

Emotions are precisely why my money approach works. Paying the minimum on installment bills tackles emotions head-on. We are acting instead of re-acting. We're tossing the bills into the backseat and saying, "Get out of my way! I've got places to go, people to see, things to do and, frankly, you are slowing me down! I'm tired of your making me depressed, crowding into first place, and keeping me outside waiting. You bills may come along for the ride because I realize you are part of living, but you will no longer run the show. I'm in charge here, and I will drive from now on!"

"Yeah," you might be saying, "I guess it's not a totally crazy idea, but it's certainly not something for me." Why do we do that? Why do we dismiss an idea that's easy, fun, and proven to work without even trying it?

Why? Because it's unfamiliar. When we're in unfamiliar territory, we begin to hesitate, put up our guard, question, challenge, and become skeptical. When I introduce "paying the minimum" in a workshop, I see, feel, and hear strong reactions all over the room. In one workshop Grant spoke up. "There's a tremendous amount of inertia in the old way of doing things. There's comfort in situations even though they're not workable."

That's for sure. Talk about the comfort of the familiar. Every single month I'd get myself all worked up with yet another burst of effort to get my bills paid off, just to have the bills come in the following month higher than ever. Dave put it so well, "Well, what I've been doing sure hasn't worked. I feel I ought to at least give Carol's idea a try."

Try paying the minimum on your credit card bills for the next six months, and get to know how and why it works so well. You'll be surprised and delighted at how much it will help you in resisting the temptation to charge. Having given this approach a try, you can decide for yourself how well it is working for you.

The "pay the minimum" idea is a pivotal one. If you dare to explore it and use it, you'll reap incredible benefits. Try it, you'll be soooooo glad you did.

WHAT DID NOT WORK FOR ME

First let me share what does not work in regard to bills. Then, I'll show you what does work and the reasons that it works. Finally, I'll try to answer every possible question and challenge to this system that you might come up with.

Every month I sat down with the bills, and every month the same thing happened. I'd open a credit card bill and look at the balance owing — let's say it was $800. I hated owing $800. I wanted the bill gone. My mind would start to calculate how to squeeze out as much as possible to get rid of this awful bill. I'd say to myself, "If we cut back, eat nothing but soup and rice, we'll have this bill paid off in no time." Then I'd write a check for $100 thinking, "Yippee! In about seven more months this bill will be paid off!" Here is what I imagined would happen.

$$
\begin{aligned}
\text{VISA bill} &= \$800.00 \\
\text{My payment} &= \underline{100.00} \\
\text{Balance still due} &= \$700.00
\end{aligned}
$$

Inside I rejoiced, saying, "In about seven months this bill will be gone!" I was going to stomp out that bill. Or was I? What was wrong with my brilliant plan? How come ten years later not only did we still have the VISA bill, but now we owed more than ever before? Because:

1) We needed that money. We were four people living on one teacher's income. I had just written a check for $100 to VISA that bought absolutely nothing for that month. (Talk about denial of reality.) It was one hundred dollars going out the door today for something bought in the past. We needed the money for food and household expenses, and I had just given it to the credit card companies.

2) We kept using our credit cards! Since I had taken $100 and bought "nothing" with it, by the twentieth or, for certain, by the twenty-fifth of the month, we were out of money. In order to buy toothpaste, batteries, soap, gas for the car, we'd have to use credit cards to get us through. Since my large payment made me feel that the bill was dwindling, I found it easy

to pull out my card and use it, saying to myself, "A couple of small charges won't hurt." Month after month, year after year, I repeated this pattern. I stayed dedicated to getting the bills paid off, and our bills kept rising. Feeling depressed about our debt and lack of money became a way of life.

The problem with my pay-off-the-bills-as-fast-as-I-can approach was that when the bill arrived the next month, it wasn't $100 less, as I had imagined it would be. In fact, it was usually even more than the month before.

Next month: VISA installment bill = $933.27

Instead of the VISA bill going down into the $700s, it arrived at over $900! Month after month I played this game of trying to pay off the bills. Meanwhile, the balance on the bills climbed. My hurry-up solution for getting rid of the bills did not work.

SUMMARY OF WHAT DOES NOT WORK

This was my pattern:

+ I'd put more money than we could afford toward the bills.

+ I wouldn't put anything into a backup emergency savings account.

+ A few weeks into the month we'd be out of money.

+ We'd have to use our credit cards to buy deodorant, envelopes, toilet paper, etc., in order to make it to the next paycheck.

+ And so it went month after month for ten years . . . pay a lot toward the bills, run out of money, buy with credit cards . . .

This approach does not work.

WHAT WORKS!

Pay the minimum amount due (and don't use the cards).

I had no idea then, but this one decision would start an incredible chain reaction that would put money in the bank, get me out of debt for good, and launch me into making my dreams come true.

With each credit card installment bill I began looking at the "minimum due." I'd read the measly little suggested minimum, glance at the total due, and *gasp*. Temporarily frozen in fear, I'd have to fight the thought that this bill would never go away. Fight the urge to write a whopping check. Fight the urge to give away the money we needed to live on now.

Gently I would remind myself of the truth. Having my bills paid off *does not* equal happiness. Having control of my money and having a plan that brings to life my dreams and goals does equal happiness.

Then I'd force myself to write a check for the minimum. Yes, force myself. Each month I had to struggle to overcome the old familiar voice trying to talk me into paying more toward the bills than we could afford.

Somehow I'd lose newly acquired perspective when I'd sit down to pay the bills. I'd forget about daily surprises, unforeseen emergencies, and our lack of savings. I'd deny the fact that we needed every penny of our paycheck just to get through the month. My mind, still hanging on to the ridiculous notion that "no bills" equals joy and fulfillment, would try to get me to put money we needed for groceries and necessities toward the bills. The new me didn't fall for it. I paid the minimum.

This was not an easy choice. It was new. It was unfamiliar. But I did it. Instead of pulling a whopping $100 out of our small checking account and sending it to VISA, I'd pay the suggested $22 minimum. With only $22 going out instead of $100 we had $78 more dollars available for windshield wiper blades, laundry soap, groceries. Best of all is that I had loosened up money so we could pay ourselves first. And in addition, with $78 more in the checkbook there was a better chance of not needing to use the card. (Since I had been paying more than the minimum on several bills, this approach freed up lots of money.)

Obviously the only possible way paying the minimum amount works is to stop using the card. Initially my grandiose plan had been the instant quick fix: never use a credit card again. Well, it may have been a great idea in theory, but it sure didn't work that easily in real life.

Each month I'd done everything I could to keep from using my credit cards. Though it had never worked before, this time it actually did. Why? Because this time I had incentive and motivation. This time I was actually putting money toward my dreams and goals and they were happening. I wasn't making these changes because I should (a guilt-inducing voice from the outside), I was choosing to put cash in my hand because I wanted to (listening to the voice from inside of me). When money did run out, I'd have to use credit, but I'd do so with much less guilt. Now I had the satisfaction of knowing I had more and more money in the bank and that I was in the process of ending the credit card dependency cycle. I was determined to unleash myself from the helpless feeling of being at the mercy of a "loan" from VISA, Sears, or some creditor to buy something. I wanted out of the credit card trap. What was new and exciting was that I didn't want to use the credit cards. What I wanted, really wanted, was the choices I would have when I had money in my name.

I wanted the freedom and the feelings of control that come with having cash. I became more and more creative and made more and more choices with my money. I was determined to arrive at the day when I didn't have to use my credit cards.

Weaning ourselves from the use of credit cards is easier said than done. If you're used to spending more than you make (as I was), then it's going to take a bit of time and some creative energy to change the tide. The key to the switch is in our awareness of the CHOICES we have. It was amazing how many things I was buying, ordering, and doing that were pure habit or reflex and didn't really bring me satisfaction or significantly increase the quality of my life.

So what do we do about the things we want but can't afford? What can we do to keep from feeling deprived? We can do as my friend Janet and her husband do. They say, "Put it on the list. We know we can't have everything, so those things we really want are on 'the list' and prioritized — but not eliminated."

As I focused more and more on my goals, such as a family trip to Great Grandma's house and Disneyland, I began paying greater attention to where I was spending money. A magazine subscription would come up for renewal, and I'd carefully question whether I wanted that money to stay in my pocket for travel or a guilt-free night out — or whether I really wanted the magazine. I began to look at *every* purchase as a choice. With that awareness came increased energy and the ability to take action — to choose what I really wanted. My new choices ended up eliminating all kinds of frivolous things and left much more money in the checkbook. With more money in the checkbook, I made it farther into the month without using credit until finally my cards were no longer in use.

Alan Cohen, in his book *The Dragon Doesn't Live Here Anymore,* explains what his friend calls the "mythical ten percent." It's the "ten percent more that if we had, we know would really satisfy us . . . the only problem is, it's always ten percent *more* than we have — no matter what we have!" Think about it. What do you own now that wasn't even on the market a few years ago? VCR? Microwave? Hot tub? CD player? Video camera? Laptop computer? And the list goes on. Every day new ideas and inventions are coming out. If we aren't focused on what we really want, before we know it we have bought the latest "in" piece of clothing or the latest holiday gadget. In the process, the musical instrument, vacation, or early retirement we've longed for all our lives goes by the wayside because our money is gone.

When we're actively pursuing our dreams, we have a reason to make wiser choices — and we do. What's marvelous is that we make wiser choices across the board. So many people have said to me, "My whole life is changing! Especially the way I spend my time. I'm taking more and more time for things I love to do."

Though it may seem that you're hooked on credit forever, hang in there. Open your eyes to all your choices each moment of the day. Label your Dream Box and get your money in there. Once you push a boulder over the edge of the cliff, there's no stopping it — and once you start there'll be no stopping you!

"But, but, but . . . ," you say.

"How about the eighteen or twenty-two percent interest I'm paying?"

That's what I thought all those years, too. After ten years of draining the paycheck dry attempting the get rid of the balance in order to save those high interest payments, do you know how much I had really saved, how much actual cash I had in the bank? Zero. Zip. None. I hadn't saved a penny by the hurry up-and-get-rid-of-the-high-interest-rate approach. Once again the theory spouted by finance experts just didn't cut it in real life. No money is saved unless we actually save it. Real money in our hand (or savings account), now *that's* money saved. (If your credit card company is charging 21 percent, make a few phone calls and have your account switched to a company that charges only 5% to 12%.)

Remember, what matters is what works. If you're sick of having no money in the bank and tired of having bills weighing you down, then do something about it. Start now to grab your change or a dollar here and two dollars there and tuck it away — for you.

One night in a workshop, as people challenged and

resisted this whole pay-the-minimum concept, Dan volunteered what he had done between classes. "I was sitting there feeling sorry for myself — paying my end-of-the-month bills — but I did pay the minimum on my credit cards. It felt good and bad. Bad because of the high interest and bad because of the feeling that I'll have this bill forever."

Notice that Dan mentioned he felt good and bad — but chose to elaborate on what was most familiar, the bad feeling. To help us begin to make the good feelings more familiar, let's take a look at all the positive effects of Dan's one decision to pay the minimum on his bills. Following are a few of the countless benefits of paying the minimum on your credit card and installment bills.

Ten powerful benefits from paying the minimum on installment bills

1. "Having more money left for me" was Dan's answer when I asked him what felt good about his choice to pay the minimum. Absolutely. That is the number one reason to pay the minimum on our installment bills — so that we have more cash for ourselves. Having money means choices and having money is the only way out of the credit card trap.

2. We're breaking the cycle. We're making the courageous choice to turn our back on what feels comfortable and familiar and take the plunge into the dark unknown of "paying the minimum."

Whether we can admit it or not, we are unconsciously locked into patterns of behaving. I remember my sixth-grade teacher, Mr. Beasley, telling us to notice that we always put the same shoe on first. I was certain he was wrong. I raised my hand and told him that I put on whichever shoe was closest. He smiled and asked us to go home and find out for ourselves. Darn. (I always put my left shoe on first!) The fact is, our habits are unconscious and ingrained. Even if they aren't working, we keep them up because they provide the comfort of what's familiar.

Breaking the get-the-bills-paid-off-as-fast-as-I-can cycle is a major step. We're going against the flow. Against what all the experts say. Against what our parents and partner and friends would advise. Without a doubt, the first time and every time you make the difficult choice to pay the minimum on your credit card bills, it is cause to celebrate! (We gave Dan a round of applause.)

Dan added, "I just want you to know that I tried really hard to be negative. I kept telling myself, 'This isn't for me because I'm overextended.' But the positive part was there. I even made a list on my desk that said, 'I know I can get cheaper auto insurance and I bet I can figure out something for health insurance and I bet I can lower the interest rate on my MasterCard by going with another MasterCard company.'"

3. Positive energy is created by the positive choice. The choice to pay the minimum is a choice to take charge of our money and our future. Our first step creates hope — an uplifting, positive feeling.

4. We're recognizing new choices. When we see new choices in one area of our life, it carries over to all of our choices — like the domino effect.

5. The positive choice to be in charge removes many of the bad feelings surrounding the bills. "I've had the impression all my life that bills aren't supposed to be fun to pay in the first place and going to work isn't supposed to be fun, either," offered Sharon. "I've grown up with the myth that life is not supposed to be fun and if it hurts it's better and if it feels bad it must be right. I started remembering some of the things I saw as a kid that my parents did with their money. The only way I learned is by what they did or didn't tell me."

Now is a perfect time to reexamine what we've been doing all these years and, perhaps for the first time in our lives, establish our own approach to bills and money. The moment we pay ourselves first, we've interjected fun into bill paying. Suddenly there's a positive, uplifting reason to go to work because work equals money earned and money equals dreams coming true.

6. We're taking control. When we're calling the shots in our own life, we feel better about ourselves, and our outlook is brighter. When we quit throwing the ball into someone else's court, and we say, "I'll take care of this myself," and we keep the ball in our court, we create feelings of power, independence, and pride in ourselves. "Much of our lives we stand waiting for the knight in shining armor," said Grant. "With this money approach, we're solving our own problems by choices we present to ourselves by ourselves. The whole concept of coming to our own rescue is quite different."

Sharon added, "If I'm taking care of me, then I have the energy and the awareness to reach out and take care of others."

7. Paying the minimum discourages us from using our credit cards. Lance expressed it so well. "If you're paying minimum payments of ten or twenty dollars, it seems like it will bug you more than using the credit card. You know if you keep using it, you'll have the bill the rest of your life. When you were paying one hundred and two hundred dollars toward the bill, you felt more free to keep using the card because you thought you were paying it off."

8. We've shifted our energy to the present. When we stop using credit and pay the minimum on our installment bills, we're living in the present. We have newfound energy that we can use for making our dreams come true.

9. We've taken away the guilt. What? No guilt? No disproportionate feelings of obligation? No obsession with the bills? What a concept! What a free and welcome feeling.

10. We've set new priorities based on what we truly value. Installment bills aren't worthy of the all-important status I gave them all those years. They're not worth strapping ourselves or perhaps our whole family for. They're not worth ruining the quality of today because we think we might feel better when they're gone. The fact is that paying a bill brings only a brief moment of relief. Before we know it, the car needs repair, the rent goes up, or the kids need new shoes. The bills are here to stay. By putting them in perspective, we can move on to putting our efforts toward achieving our goals.

Check it out: ten life-giving benefits as a result of one choice, one action, one decision — the decision to pay the minimum on our credit card bills.

In one workshop Bobby asked, "Do you have a little chart

or something to explain this? I went home last week and tried to explain it to my wife, and she doesn't buy it. She looks at the interest rate and the big bill and says it doesn't make sense to pay the minimum." "She's right," I told Bobby, "it doesn't. It would be like trying to explain falling in love. We are looking for logical $2 + 2 = 4$ simplicity in an extremely complex and deeply emotional issue: money management." (Afterward, Bobby's wife listened to audio tapes of the workshop. Three months later this note arrived: "We have all of our accounts set up and the process seems to be working. Heather took to it like a fish to water. Thank you very much.")

Some thoughts for those who "share" money and expenses. Anytime there are two people, there are two different philosophies or two different sets of learned behaviors on managing money. You may be questioning whether it's possible for things to change if your partner doesn't read this book or chooses to reject the whole concept. The answer is yes. When I was married, my husband never did accept this approach to money management. Over the years, others have told me of clever and creative means they came up with to get money for their dreams — even in the face of a resistant or controlling partner.

If you are trying to cope with a partner who tends to spend all available money, you may want to try saving money in a retirement account (IRA, tax-sheltered annuity, 401(k), Keogh, and so on). Your partner may be less likely to withdraw money that is earmarked for retirement. One reason may be because there's a penalty for early withdrawal. What made the difference in my situation was that I took my energy away from trying to control my partner's spending and, instead, put energy into figuring out ways to get money in the bank. Don't give up just because your partner won't go along. Be creative and find a way to start saving.

Dan wondered, "But isn't that worse, to just watch your partner keep driving the credit card bills up and up?" It wasn't for me. When my energy was tied up in a futile attempt to control my partner's spending, there was nothing positive going on. Once I began saving money, I had the satisfying and increasingly secure feeling of knowing we finally had savings that were building. Over the next ten years, our family of four living on one income accumulated over $30,000 in tax-sheltered savings. (The regular monthly deposits, plus the compound interest, made the money grow rapidly. In the next chapter we talk about the power of a lump sum of money. By the time there is $30,000 saved, even if you don't deposit any money into the account, at 4 percent interest the account will continue to grow by $1,200 each year *all by itself!*)

"It's just starting to register," said Bobby. "You can pay bills and still live a life where you're not a slave to your check-book. And that doesn't mean you're out just blowing money and being irresponsible. Somehow I feel that if I'm not slaving over it and making it a big pain in the rear, then I'm being irresponsible."

Exactly. Isn't that what happened when I brought up the idea of paying the minimum? "But that's so irresponsible!" Once again the brain jumped to the wrong conclusion because it forgot to take our emotions into account.

I interviewed Kate about a year after she took my money workshop. Notice how the long-term solution of paying the minimum helped Kate and her partner in the short term. Even though they're not even close to being out of debt, they're living and enjoying life more and feel in control. Kate: "You know that stuff you talked about was really true for us. One of us was in school and one of us wasn't. No matter what our financial situation, it seemed like we never had enough. And then suddenly, we had! Once we started saving money, we found we had enough to pay the bills *and* save money — which we never thought we could do before.

"We have learned to live on the money we have, even though we're in big debt, like owing twenty thousand dollars on credit cards. Psychologically what helps, though, is that we have several savings accounts, each designated for different things. One account is to have at least three months' living expenses; we're building that one up. And then we have another one that is long-term savings and investments kind of stuff. The other one is probably for buying a house, because I think we really want to do that. And the other one is for the car — for everything related to the car."

I asked Kate, "With that much debt, why aren't you feeling overwhelmed and depressed?"

"I think the main reason is because we have money in savings. We are paying the smallest amount we can on the bills. (We had to do some compromising around that because I wanted to pay the absolute minimum and my partner didn't want to do that, so we agreed on a compromise.) The other difference is that when I got out of that class, I started looking at other things. For example, I switched some of our credit cards to companies with lower interest rates because some of our credit cards were really high — one charged nineteen percent and the other twenty-one percent interest.

"You know, we used to pay our bills and not look at the total due because it was so frightening, especially if we had charged, because we were back up again and then some. So now when we pay our bills, we know they're going away! I know exactly how much debt we are in, and before, I just didn't want to look at it. I'm out of denial about it, but I also feel like now I have a tool to get out of debt. Today we're in a place where we have come to an agreement and we follow certain guidelines; we also watch our savings grow and we get really excited about that. We bought a book and a ledger and we keep track of our savings growing, and that is really fun to see. We send an extra twenty here and an extra twenty there when we can."

Paying the minimum works because we are choosing to make our bills unimportant and paying ourselves paramount. But accepting this approach is tough. Our minds won't quit resisting the idea long enough to try it. Those who do take charge and heave the installment bills into the backseat and invite their dreams and goals up front will experience a shift that carries through their entire life.

See if this next situation has a familiar ring. When Leslie came for help, her greatest concern was her $7,000 plus MasterCard bill. It was a bit tricky to get her to talk about her life and her personal goals because the weight of the bills was heavy on her mind. After some coaxing she finally began talking about herself. She expressed her contentment with a quiet, rather routine life made up of work and meeting friends for a movie or dinner out from time to time. Although it was obvious Leslie was sincere and was talking openly about herself, I had a strong feeling there was more and so gently asked a few more questions to see where it would lead.

As she talked, a smile came across her face. She came to life as she realized how much she longs to travel with her friends on their weekend getaway trips. But before she got too excited she remembered her MasterCard bill and said, "I can't possibly relax and have fun until the MasterCard bill is handled. I would be acting so irresponsibly."

When I suggested that she list the goals that would make up her money plan, she listed:

Emergency account

Emergency future (unemployment, change of residence)

Weekend-getaway-with-friends account

Car account

Christmas account

As we looked at the list, I pointed out that four of the five accounts were duty-oriented and that the plan didn't include much fun for building anticipation into day-to-day life. I asked, "Is there any chance you would change the plan you just mapped out if you had no MasterCard bill?"

Leslie thought for a long, long time. "I suppose it would," she finally said. "If I didn't owe seven thousand dollars on my credit card, then I could consider the trip to Europe I've always wanted."

Another surprise! She had begun the session by saying she was content with her life as it was and that her only issue was her large credit card debt. She wasn't aware that what she really wanted was to be going on weekend getaway trips with her friends and planning a trip to Europe. The truth was obscured by the bills.

After all these years I'm still surprised at the grip the bills can have. When I asked Leslie if her plan would change if she had no MasterCard bill, I honestly expected her to respond immediately, "Of course not." I'm still in awe when I see the blinding power of bills. I wonder if maybe something like this was going on in Leslie's mind:

"Let's see. Would I have any other goals if I didn't have a MasterCard bill?

"But I do have a MasterCard bill! I not only have a MasterCard bill, I have a monstrous one. I owe over seven thousand dollars!"

Pause. Back to the question.

"What did she just ask me? Would I have any *other* goals if I didn't have a MasterCard bill?

"How can I answer that?! I *do* have a MasterCard bill."

Pause.

"Let's see. Would I have any other goals or dreams I'd be pursuing if I weren't so consumed with my bills? Oh. Wait a minute. France, Italy, Switzerland. I'd almost forgotten!"

Have your bills kept you from knowing what you love most? Are you waiting at the threshold of the bridge, telling yourself, "I can't cross until my bills are paid"?

The bottom line in Leslie's story is that the zip was missing in her life. Her reason to bound out of bed and grab life by the tail had fizzled out. My hunch is that she had become infected with the same "poor me" syndrome I had, and she'd been using the same destructive drug (credit cards) to attempt to cure her ills. When we don't have a steady dose of fun and anticipation built into our lives, one day looks pretty much the same as the next. So how do we cope with the drudgery? We treat ourselves. Out comes our credit card as we soothe our boredom with an espresso, new clothes, or dinner with a friend.

How did Leslie's bill get up to $7,000? How did yours or mine? For most of us it crept up in our rush to pay it off.

THE CHOICE TOM HAD THAT MOST OF US DON'T

One day I answered my office phone and heard this inspiring story.

"Hi. My name is Tom and I took your class about a year and a half ago. Since then I've saved over thirteen thousand dollars, and I'm needing help in making a big decision." (He'd saved thirteen thousand dollars in a year and a half? He had my attention!) Tom had found a prime piece of lakefront property for sale. He wasn't sure about buying it and wanted to talk it over.

As you can imagine, I was itching to know the rest of the story, so I asked him what his financial situation was a year and a half before when he attended my workshop. "When I took your class, I had no money in savings and several thousand in credit card debt. I began my money plan with four accounts with five dollars each, and then I went down a month later and opened up a couple more with five dollars. I just slowly started. It felt good when I opened those accounts because I was organizing my money. You know, I had a checking and a savings account for fifteen or twenty years, and I'd move money back and forth from savings to checking so many times. It was always month-to-month, scraping by. I did that for so long. It was nice when I opened those accounts.

"Then I started writing checks for twenty and thirty dollars and dropping them in one account or another. I got some bonuses at work, and I put that into my accounts. About six months after your workshop, I got a ten percent bonus, and I put that away. Then I realized that what I really wanted was to quit my job, so I did and got another job. Now, instead of paying large amounts of money to all those creditors — you know, VISA and all that stuff — I pay it to myself!

"Right now I'm putting eight hundred dollars a month away. You see, I'm putting about four hundred in those four different accounts, and that's for travel, education, emergencies now, and emergencies later. I also put four hundred dollars into saving for the house."

I interrupted to ask Tom, "How did that feel?"

"It was nice. Real nice. I mean, it's just a real good feeling to have all the money set up where I want for the things I really want."

Tom explained that the owner of the piece of property he was considering buying was asking $10,000 down and $900 a month for four years. The math was easy. After the down payment, Tom would still have $3,000 left. Since he was already putting $800 into his savings accounts each month, the $900 payment would be doable. But, as always, this was primarily an emotional decision. Our time on the phone was spent discussing his values and what would bring him the most satisfaction in the long run. In the end he decided it wasn't where he wanted to place his money and energy at this point in his life.

After our conversation I had a clearer picture than ever of the difference between cash on hand and a pocketful of credit cards. Tom's cash gave him the power of choices. He could toss around the idea of whether or not to purchase prime lakefront property, while most of us would have passed right by the For Sale sign because buying the land wasn't an option. All the credit cards in the world wouldn't have bought the land. Tom, however, had a choice because he had cash.

QUESTIONS AND CHALLENGES TO THE "MINIMUM" CONCEPT

✦ **But what about all that interest I'm paying?** Remember, we don't really *save* the interest money when we pay our bills off quickly. In order to truly save money we must actually squirrel it away into a sock or savings account. Our real problem is not the interest we're paying; it's that we don't have cash on hand.

A piece of good news. When we begin paying ourselves, as well as everyone else, we'll finally have our money earning interest. So even though we may be paying 12% interest charges on our credit cards, we're beginning to offset that charge with the money we're saving. For example, if our saved money is earning 3% interest and we're paying 12% on credit cards, we're not only giving ourselves the power that comes with having cash, we've also reduced our interest charges to just 9%.

✦ **"But I'll have this bill forever."** Not true. Once again our mind, panicking at this unfamiliar new way to approach credit card debt, jumps to an exaggerated conclusion: "I'll have this bill forever." This information triggers despair, urgency, and countless other feelings. The fact is, we made the choice along the way to charge items we couldn't really afford, and now it's time to find an effective way to deal with the situation we've got ourselves into. It's time to reprogram the mind with new information. If we don't charge on our credit cards, and we do pay the minimum payment each month — they go away. "Initially, the idea of paying the minimum sounded so stupid," said Carl. "But then I realized it gave me more money to get through the month, and then I didn't have to charge anymore. It feels great to be out of debt."

✦ **If I get a raise or have a little extra money, shouldn't I put that money toward the bills?** Just remember that whenever we want to pay extra on the bills, we're hooked. The question to ask ourselves is always the same: "How much money do I have?" Before we can consider parting with our hard-earned cash, we need to stop and ask ourselves how much we have on hand. "Is there plenty of money for daily surprises like car repairs, a stereo that goes on the blink, kids who need money for a school event, or perhaps a dentist's or doctor's bill? Is there ample money in my emergency future account (explained in Chapter 6) in case of injury or unemployment?" And how about our dreams? Are we experiencing the excitement and anticipation of making them come true? How long have they been on hold? When my son's fourteen-year-old friend and classmate died last summer, we were reminded once again that all we have is now, and that each moment is precious. Let's put the bills on simmer, not life.

✦ **But what if each month I faithfully pay off the balance on my credit cards?** Once again, there's no right or wrong. What we're driving at is a mode of operation that is deeply satisfying and gives us a strong sense of control over our lives. What happened in my case is that for a couple of years my former husband and I had two incomes, no children, and a ninety-five-dollar-a-month rent payment. Every month we'd charge several hundred dollars' worth of merchandise, and every month I'd easily pay it off. We were in the habit of taking today's money to pay for last month's purchases.

Our lives changed when our first child arrived; we bought a home and began living on one income. What didn't change was our habit of charging. Now when the credit card bills arrived, there wasn't enough money to pay them off. We continued our pattern of charging and our debt began to mount. Is it possible that with a few emergencies or a change in lifestyle you, too, wouldn't be able to pay off your credit card bills? And, besides, do we want to take today's money and spend it to pay for something we bought in the past?

✦ **"But I want to pay off all my bills so I can start with a clean slate."** Be careful. Too often when we have important paperwork, what do we do instead? We spend an hour organizing, answering notes to friends (cleaning the slate), and suddenly it's late, we're sleepy, and we head for bed. The problem? We can't sleep. Instead of doing what needed to be done — writing the important letter or paying the bills — we fooled ourselves and cleaned the desk.

I'll never forget what Elaine said at the first money workshop I ever presented. "You know," she said, "I could sell some stock and pay off my installment bills, but I'm not going to. That would be an escape to a 'quick fix,' and I might not learn my lesson. It took a long time for me to charge up all that debt. I actually want that monthly credit card bill to remind me of the trap I never want to be in again."

✦ **"You keep talking about the importance of feeling good. Well, I'll feel real good and have lots of inner**

---

satisfaction when the #!@% bills are out of my hair!"
Again we need to bring the mind back into perspective. Often
when we look at a credit card bill, life stops for the moment
and all we see is the balance owing. With that dollar amount
our only focus, we are drawn like a magnet into its grip. All
we can think of is how to get the bill paid off. The power of
credit card debt is enormous. We lose all perspective. Lynn had
a credit card bill that was down to only eighty-five dollars
owed. She told us she really, really wanted to just pay it off but
didn't because she was afraid to come to class and admit she
had paid more than the minimum. "As I struggled with what
to do, I began to realize that Christmas is just six weeks away,
and I don't have any money in savings."

Get up from your bill-paying chair and walk around. Remind yourself of the bigger picture of life. Are you being
tempted to give money to the installment bills that you need
for necessities and emergencies?

✦ **But I don't think I can feel in control unless my
credit cards are paid off.** Melissa wrote, "I feel more relieved and lighter than I thought possible. I always thought I
would have to be out of debt before I felt in control. I actually
chuckled when I wrote a check to my credit card company
for fifteen dollars. I always felt so childish before — now I feel
my age."

Try this. Imagine you have three million dollars that is all
yours. Notice for just a moment how secure that feels. You no
longer have to go to work, and the things you've always
wanted to do and have are possible. Now, with three million
cash in hand, think about your bills. What's happened to the
tension and feeling of urgency to get them paid off? Though

the example is extreme, it helps give us perspective. First we must pay ourselves and get some money in hand. Once we have money, the bills lose their power — the hurry is gone.

✦ **What's wrong with carrying credit cards if I don't use them?** It's not a matter of "wrong" or "right," it's a matter of what works. Only you know whether you can handle having approved credit. The key is to stop fooling ourselves and find a solution that works for us. Almost all of our obstacles are the ones we have put there. It's time for each of us to look in the mirror and tell the truth. Can I carry cards and not use them? The point is to do what we need to do to make certain we succeed in reaching our goals. For some of us that means not having or carrying credit cards.

✦ **"But what if I put just a little extra toward the bills each month . . . maybe just ten or twenty dollars more?"** Give a little more money to *whom?* If we're so eager to get rid of our hard-earned money, why don't we pay something extra to ourselves! And besides, is that really "extra" money? Money that isn't or won't be needed for anything? Is the money there to handle family emergencies, car repair, holidays, wedding gifts, and household maintenance expenses? Do we really have extra, or are we in the grip of the bills once again? We need to listen carefully to the words we are choosing — are we really saying what we mean?

How did Tom save $13,000 in a year and a half? He paid himself the extra little amounts, not the bills. Why are we so quick to give away our money? Keep it. Keep it for you. Keep it for your dreams, emergencies, kids, security, retirement. Here's the question to always ask yourself when you're feeling compelled to pay extra on the bills: "Do I have six months' salary saved? Do I have more than enough cash on hand to cover any and all emergencies? Are my dreams coming true?" When we can say yes to each question, *then* if there is extra money, we can decide whether we want to put it toward the bills.

If you are tempted to pay more than the minimum, *always, always, always* ask yourself, "How much do I have in savings?" "If tomorrow the car needs a new transmission, is there cash to pay for it?" "If the refrigerator quits or I'm injured and can't work for the next three months, is there money available to meet my needs?"

The question isn't "Can I pay more than the minimum?" The key question here is "How much do I have in savings?" Keep remembering, money is an *emotional* issue. With all the financial advisers out there, why aren't we all masters at managing our money? Because managing money isn't about numbers. It isn't about being debt free and it isn't about saving money. Managing money is about zeroing in on our values. It's about managing how we feel. It's about motivation. Managing money is about continually sifting out the unimportant and focusing on what really matters. It's about giving ourselves a reason to jump out of bed.

FACT: If you don't use your credit cards and if you do pay the minimum payment each month, those bills will disappear. Guaranteed.

FACT: Taking the focus off the installment bills and concentrating on what turns us on in life works. Thousands have chosen to make this happen for themselves, though probably not one of them believed any of this the first time they heard it.

PAYING ALL THE BILLS ONE TIME A MONTH

Paying all the bills at the same time each month is a tremendous tool — those who make the effort to learn how will reap big-time rewards.

One of the greatest gifts a company can give its employees is to pay them once a month.

You might be saying:

"I can't possibly pay all my bills at the same time, because I get paid every week."

"I'm on commission and the amount of my checks varies."

"I'm in a business where some months I have big checks, and others I have no money coming in at all."

"My bills arrive at all different times of the month. This won't work."

"I pay the bills as they come in. I can't stand having them around."

Can't. Almost every time we use the word "can't," what we really mean is, "I don't want to." It's understandable that we don't want to pay the bills once a month because it has probably seemed impossible — until now.

Paying the bills once a month is like the difference between taking a covered wagon to visit your best friend a thousand miles away and hopping on an airplane. Instead of dreading the mail each day and constantly playing the money-juggling act all month long — it's all handled at once. When you take care of your entire money matters at one time each month, you can kick back and relax — you're under control. You've paid yourself first by putting money toward your goals, and you've paid your bills (the minimum on your installment debt). As you'll learn in Chapter 6, you'll get the boost of actually seeing your money growing as each month you deposit money for your goals and write in the total you've saved on your Master Money Plan sheet (pages 188–189). Once you've learned how, you'll understand why people tell me, "Carol, I never would have believed it, but bill paying is actually fun! I really look forward to paying myself and watching my goals coming true, and I love seeing the installment bills getting smaller and smaller. Everything is under control, and it only takes a couple of hours once each month."

There are basically two ways to tackle paying your bills once a month. The method you choose will depend on how and when you get paid.

First I'll address those who get paid on a regular basis, where the amount of the paycheck(s) each month is fairly predictable. Then I'll discuss the approach for those who are paid on commission, work for themselves, work at a seasonal job, or for whatever reason have a widely varying amount of money to deal with each month.

Method 1: If you're paid a predictable amount each month

Begin by getting the facts. Total the amounts of all the paychecks you receive in any one month. For example:

1st	=	$900
15th	=	$900
Total income for the month	=	$1,800

Next, place your total income for the month at the top of a page and subtract each bill in order of priority: your goals first, then rent, and so on, with the installment bills where they belong, at the bottom of the heap.

Total income for the month	**=**	**$1,800.00**
My goals	=	$ 32.00
Rent/mortgage	=	650.00
Health/doctor/dentist	=	129.00
Heat	=	70.00
Electricity	=	52.00
Water/sewer/garbage	=	55.00
Car insurance	=	70.00
Telephone	=	48.00
MasterCard (minimum)	=	62.00
Sears (minimum)	=	38.00
Dept. store credit card (minimum)	=	41.00
Balance	=	$553.00

The $553 is the amount of money left for the entire month (for food, clothes, supplies . . .). It's an automatic budget. With all the income for the month listed and *all* the known bills subtracted — we know exactly how much money is left for the entire month. We've stopped the anxiety of the mind game that tricks us by saying, "Don't worry, another check's coming in just a couple of days." What we see is what we've got. Food, batteries, gasoline, birthday expenses, clothes, shampoo, dog food, breath mints, you name it — it all has to come out of the amount that is left because that's it until next month's paychecks.

Relief and a real sense of control are what we get when we do this. The craziness stops. The games stop. There it is. We bring in x amount of money and x amount goes out to pay the bills — the remainder is our automatic limit for the month.

What to do if all your bills don't arrive within the same week

Whether the bills have arrived or not, sit down with your checkbook on approximately the same date each month. You know what your regular bills are, and you know approximately what you will owe. Go ahead and enter your total pay for the month, and then pencil in each bill and subtract it from the total (as in the previous example). The amount left is reality — the actual dollars left to live on for the rest of the month. Many people write all the checks for the month at once but don't mail them until the paychecks have arrived to cover the checks written.

Although it's a challenge, it is well worth the effort to juggle your paychecks and bills around for a few months until you've managed to accumulate the paychecks to where the total is enough to pay all the bills at once. (Some people have told me they borrowed money to get started.) The peace of mind that comes with paying all the bills at one sitting during the month is more than worth the effort. (If you have a bill or two that come in at odd times of the month, call and ask the company to change your billing date.)

T. J. wrote, "I'm so excited. Our number one goal is to pay

bills once a month. We've begun this month. We're saving all our paychecks this month, and I'll sit down and pay all the bills the first of next month. I'm using a portion of our IRS return to tide us over this month while we save all the paychecks. We have several other areas we're working on, too. Change takes time. I've been working on it several years since I took your class the first time."

Once we see how little money is left after subtracting all the bills, we're usually drawn to examine our expenses more closely. We look at cable TV, magazines, newspapers, cellular phone, new car payment, club memberships, and so on, to see if this is the way we really want to spend our money. If we don't like our lack of money, we can choose to do something about it. One thing is certain: if we stop using our credit cards, the credit card debt will disappear. In time, the money that used to go out the door to pay for something we bought in the past will now be available to meet the needs of today and help plan and save for tomorrow. In the case of the itemized expenses on page 100, it would mean an extra $141!

Another bonus is that communication within the family gets a boost and overspending slows down when we pay the bills once a month. When other members of the family want to buy such and such, now we can open the checkbook and show them the bottom line: "There's forty-six dollars in checking and ten days left in the month." Case closed. But that doesn't mean anyone has to feel deprived. If the item is really important, just label a new Dream Box and go for it.

Whether we sit down and pay our bills all at once or pay them piecemeal through the month, they cost exactly the same. What isn't the same is how we feel. Scrambling to pay them here and there fills us with fear, anxiety, and worry. Paying everything at once means getting a handle on the big picture. The result? Satisfaction and control.

There's no sweat, no panic. Everything's under control. Everything has been taken care of.

Method 2: How to pay all your bills once a month if you're paid on commission, work for yourself, work at a seasonal job, or for whatever reason have a widely varying amount of money to deal with each month

First, grab the checkbook and a blank sheet of paper and make a list of all the bills you pay each month. Total them. (Don't forget to start with the money you pay yourself first.) This total is how much money you need to have each month just to get the bills paid. Add to that total the amount you usually spend on food, laundry soap, and other essentials for the month. (Guesstimate if you don't have accurate records.) This number is your baseline for how much money you need to have each month to cover basic expenses. Knowing how much money you need each month, you can begin to give yourself a predictable monthly salary.

Let's say you work on commission and bring in $6,243 dollars one month and then have no money coming in for the next two months. Let's also say that you have established that your "salary" needs to be $1,866 each month. On bill-paying day you take exactly $1,866 from your savings account and transfer it to checking. You have given yourself the peace of mind that comes with knowing you have a predictable monthly paycheck. Each day throughout the month you feel relaxed and in control, knowing you've paid yourself and all your bills.

Whether you're a dance instructor collecting small

checks throughout the month or a construction contractor dealing periodically with large sums, your goal is the same: to give yourself a predetermined baseline monthly salary.

The main benefits of paying bills once a month are:

1. Bill paying becomes fun as we look forward to the one time a month when all our money matters are taken care of, the time when we pay ourselves and step closer to reaching our goals.

2. We've set automatic controls. We deposit our once-a-month "paycheck," we pay ourselves first, and we pay the minimum due on our bills — whatever is left is it for the month.

3. With our installment bills carefully placed at the bottom of the pile of bills, we're not so tempted to pay more than the minimum due.

4. We're much more apt to live within our means. We're not as likely to overspend by fooling ourselves and saying, "Another check is just around the corner."

5. As we add money to our goals on this one day each month, we get the inner boost of actually seeing our money building on our Master Money Plan sheet (see pages 188–189) while at the same time watching our installment bill balances dwindle.

6. Peace of mind. Once we establish a routine of paying ourselves and our bills once a month, we can relax. All the

bills are paid, our installment debt starts to disappear, and we've begun achieving our goals. We've given ourselves the priceless gift that accompanies being in control of our lives and our money — peace of mind.

What if I operate on an all-cash basis?

The same suggestions apply if you operate solely with cash. Keep stashing money away until you've accumulated enough to cover paying yourself first and then all the monthly bills. (Since cash on hand can be tempting, be sure to use your genius and creativity to keep from "borrowing" from yourself.)

If one of the reasons you're on a "cash only" basis is that creditors are after your bank accounts, consider having a friend or relative (someone you trust totally) open a savings account for you with money you provide. That way your goals accounts can be earning interest.

Should I consolidate all my bills?

The decision whether to consolidate or not is arrived at by carefully considering what will be most empowering and advantageous to you in the long run.

One of the biggest dangers of getting a consolidation loan to pay off all of our smaller bills is that now we're walking around with credit cards in our pocket that have a zero balance. With nothing owing on our credit cards, it's easy to become tempted. We're out shopping and we start to think, "Gosh, just *one* charge won't hurt. I'll pay it off as soon as the bill arrives." Before we know it, we're off and running — one charge leads to another. We end up paying a huge consolidation loan each month *as well as* payments on all our cards! Holly and Chris inherited $6,000 and used all the money to pay off their credit cards. They said they were at the workshop because they had already charged their credit cards right back up to the limit.

Banks and credit unions are competing for your interest dollars and are always listing the advantages of consolidating. One ad I got in the mail said, "Sometimes one bill just makes more sense." They talk about the ease of only writing one check and how they'll "take care of it for you." Sound familiar? The knight in shining armor arriving with a quick fix, ready to take care of us and eliminate our money troubles.

We're no longer interested in a quick fix that is soon to fail. Now we're after the long-term, *permanent* solution — a way out of the credit card trap once and for all. When I first decided to pay only the minimum on our installment debt, we had about seven different credit card bills. It was something like this:

Credit Card	Balance Due	Minimum Payment	Months until Gone
Major credit card	$3,600	$108	33
Major credit card	2,700	81	33
Department store	1,300	80	16
Department store	800	80	10
Department store	400	20	20
Department store	350	50	7
Department store	230	40	6

Two things happen when we stop using our credit cards and begin faithfully to pay the minimum amount due: 1) bit by bit the minimum payments drop, thus putting more money in our pockets, and 2) sooner than we thought possible, we start receiving windfalls as, one by one, our bills are paid off. In the example above, the department store bill with a balance of $230 will be paid off in about six months, and that means $40 more staying at home. When a bill is finally paid off, carefully *diversify* this newfound money — perhaps putting another ten dollars toward goals and leaving the remaining thirty in the checkbook to help get through the month without charging. (Chapter 4 explains diversifying.)

By paying the minimum payment on our bills ourselves (instead of consolidating), we will have many opportunities to make decisions with our money. Each time another bill bites the dust, we have more money in our pocket and another chance to practice diversifying and managing our money. Each month as the minimum amount due decreases and cash available for the month increases, our spirits are renewed. Just as we slowly lost control over the years, now we're purposefully taking our time to gain control once again. We are in charge. This is empowerment.

Credit-Card and Bill-Paying Tips

✦ **The bank statement:** When the bank statement arrives, my goal is to balance the checkbook within two or three days so I don't end up doing it the day I pay myself and the bills. Balancing the checkbook is done only to make sure we or the bank haven't made any errors. Once your Master Money Plan (Chapter 6) is in place, you'll be looking forward to bill-paying day because you'll be watching the money you pay yourself grow in addition to celebrating the gradual disappearance of your installment bills. The idea is not to mix the chore of reconciling the bank statement with the fun of celebrating our progress.

✦ **Pay by phone.** If bill paying by phone or some other automatic bill-paying system sounds appealing to you, then look into it. Martha explained that the act of sitting down with the checkbook, writing checks, and licking stamps is traumatic and nearly unbearable for her. She said that using a bill-paying-by-phone method was one of the greatest gifts she's ever given herself. "It's over in seconds, they are open twenty-four hours, and what it has done for my sanity is incredible."

✦ **Prioritizing:** When you sit down to pay your bills, try stacking them in the order of what matters most. After putting yourself on the very tip-top of the pile, then what? Probably next come doctors, dentists, rent/mortgage payment, and so on, until way down at the very bottom of the pile sit the credit card and installment bills.

A great bonus of our setting priorities is that it'll be a cinch to pay the minimum on the credit card bills. By the time we've paid ourselves and all the other bills, there's hardly any money left for the month, and the temptation to pay more than the minimum is gone.

✦ **Filing:** One of the best things I ever did was to label a file folder Bills to Pay. When a bill arrives, I merely drop it into the file (which remains the very first folder in the file cabinet). I don't think about it, worry about it, or wonder what to do with it. The folder continues to fill until sometime between the fifth and the eighth of the month, when I pull out the folder, prioritize, pay myself, pay the bills, and fill out my Master Money Plan sheet. (See pages 188–189.)

✦ **What to do when you can't even pay the minimum:** What I have come to understand from people who work for credit rating bureaus and bill collection agencies is that creditors are most concerned that we pay them something. They say *never* to put all your bills in a hat and draw out just a few — always pay everyone something.

So, if you're swamped and can't even pay the minimum, try writing a letter to all your credit companies. In your letter explain briefly that you are in over your head and that you are reading and learning how to get back in control. *Carefully* take stock of your whole financial situation before you act. If you decide to write these letters, you must make every effort to set up a comprehensive plan that will really set you straight.

For example, let's say the minimum payment on one of your bills is $85 a month. The tendency for a lot of us is to think, "If I cut the family back to bread and water and our only entertainment is playing cards, I bet we could get by with a $70 payment." Watch out. Paying a mere $15 less each month won't put enough money in your pocket to change the tide.

Remember, the only way to really get all the way out of the credit card trap is to have money, money, money. Your plan must ensure three things: 1) that your minimum payment is low enough that you can meet it, 2) that you have enough money for day-to-day expenses so you'll no longer use the charge cards, and 3) that you're now socking money away to get yourself permanently out of the trap.

If you decide you need to go the route of writing to your creditors, you'll be asking to take an $85 monthly payment down to $10 or $15 (and, of course, you'll assure the company that you'll no longer be using the card). Being realistic is what's key. If you want out, you'll have to open the door, not just crack a window.

My friend Marcia, whose husband is a physician in private practice, told me she spends every Monday morning calling people who haven't been paying their doctor's bill. I sheepishly admitted I had mailed only $5 to my dentist that very month. "That's great!" she said, "I have no problem as long as people send us *something.*"

✦ **Watch out for two-cycle billing.** Look on your credit card disclosure and information sheet under the heading Balance Calculation Method for Purchases. What you want to see is that the finance charge is calculated based on the average daily balance, not two-cycle billing. Two-cycle billing calculates interest charges in the costliest way possible.

✦ **Treat credit card and car loan balances the same.** Have you ever noticed that it's not a major problem to pay the exact "minimum" payment on a car loan or mortgage payment? We sign a contract and agree we'll pay x amount each month until the house or car is paid for. See if it helps to place credit card bills on the same status as the car payment — paying only the minimum.

✦ **Stop fooling ourselves.** Beth had over $20,000 worth of credit card bills. Her entire check went to pay the minimum amount due on the installment bills, and she and her husband lived on his paycheck. In our private session I invited Beth to pull out her credit cards and consider cutting up just one. She nervously thumbed through the pile. "Well," she finally said, "I guess I could cut up the Sears card because we hardly ever use it except for things like tires, a new furnace, or a washing machine." Oops. Of all the cards in the huge pile, that was the very one to keep. Department store credit cards will be of little use if you're out of money and need a new hot water tank, your car repaired, or a new roof for your home. As you wean yourself from credit card use and build your own savings, hang on to a major credit card in case an emergency arises before you're equipped to pay for it.

SUMMARY

Why should anyone pay only the minimum payment due on his or her installment bills instead of getting them paid off as fast as possible and eliminating those high finance charges? Two main reasons. One is to diffuse the emotional grip bills have over us by putting them in last place, making them unimportant. The other is to free up money so we can begin to pay ourselves. Paying the minimum on the bills is a tremendous boost in moving us from the credit card trap to the freedom of choice that comes with having money.

FACT: When you take your focus off the bills and pay the minimum, the installment bills *do* go away.

FACT: You can do it.

FACT: Paying the minimum will make you want to quit using the cards and start living in the present.

FACT: By choosing to pay the minimum on your credit card bills, you are taking action that says, "My goals and I are more important than the bills." You have taken charge.

When you're tempted to pay more than the minimum, remember to ask yourself these four questions:

1. Is my emergency savings fund as substantial as it needs to be to handle a series of unexpected expenses?

2. If I put a bundle toward the bills today and found out tomorrow I had 6 weeks to live, would I want my money back?

3. Do I have at least six months' salary put away, readily available for unknown future emergencies?

4. Have I reached all my goals? Am I putting away as much as I'd like each month for the adventures I've always wanted?

Our challenge is to challenge ourselves. At the end of life do we want to be reminiscing and recall only that "By golly, we always did pay off our bills" *or* do we want to relish joyful memories of places traveled and experiences shared?

It's not the bills that are our real problem. The real culprit is our misdirected focus. Our call is to direct our energy to the very essence of what gives our life meaning. We're placing our goals in first place while easing away from the intensity of the bills. As we claim control of our money and our lives we assume the even pace of the tortoise — paying only the minimum on the installment bills — and directing our energy, enthusiasm, *and money* toward what brings us life.

FOUR

How to Divide Up $5?
You're Kidding!

It's not what happens to you,
it's what you do about it.
— W. Mitchell

*S*AVING money is boring.

Imagine sitting around with a few friends when one leaps up and says, "I know! Let's save money." "Huh?" you'd all say, thinking your friend was nuts. But if the same person jumped up and suggested, "Let's all rent a cabin!" now we've got expressions of enthusiasm. How soon? Where shall we go? To the ocean or mountains? As the event materializes they're eager to sock away money — suddenly saving is exciting.

When I left home at eighteen, I knew that I should save money. I also knew I should floss every day, I should exercise regularly, I should eat lots of fruit and vegetables, I should, I should, I should. Boring. From time to time, I would half-heartedly put some money in a savings account (operating mostly out of guilt). But since there was no plan for the money, I could take it out easily for almost any reason, and I did.

So what switches saving money from a boring "have to" to an enthusiastic "want to"? *Motivation.* When we're pursuing our goals and our dreams are coming true, the fun and satisfaction keep revitalizing us. Instead of guilt and responsibility weighing us down, we're uplifted and catapulted forward by our energy, focus, and sense of purpose.

"I've been motivated lots of times," you're saying, "but before long I seem to lose enthusiasm and fizzle out." A major reason that happens to us is that we're too vague about what we want. For example, if I ask, "Would you like some dessert?" your mind analyzes the question something like this. "Do I want dessert? Hmmmmm. Well, I'm sort of full but on the other hand, depending on what it is, I might be up for it." And then you're likely to ask, "What kind of dessert are you offering?" The vague question about dessert triggered no emotional reaction. Only your brain was put to work thinking and researching.

Now contrast that unmotivating question with this one. "How would you like a taste of the richest, most delicious and irresistible chocolate dessert ever created?" (Replace chocolate, if need be, with lemon or raspberry or whatever is your all-time favorite.) Your mouth starts to water, your nose and tongue, tantalized by the thought, eagerly await the heavenly scent and scintillating flavor.

There is a huge and vitally important lesson for us to learn from these two drastically different responses. The key is giving our emotional self something specific to respond to. Here's another example. "I'm saving for a vacation." Since the word "vacation" is nonspecific, nothing is stimulated inside of us and our brain responds with "Ho hum, so what." Compare that to "I'm going to France to relax on the Riviera, have my picture taken at the Eiffel Tower, and mingle with the French people." France as a specific vacation destination stimulates us to envision sights and sounds and fills us with eagerness and anticipation. When I finally caught on to how boring I had made saving money, I understood why I didn't have any.

In a workshop Lynn mentioned "a trip across the country" as her goal. She sighed, signifying that she was not the least bit excited. She kept saying, "I really do want to go, but I'm just not enthusiastic about saving for it." About a week later Lynn called just to share her experience, with the hope that it might help someone reading this book. What she finally realized was that the words "cross-country trip" triggered thoughts of long, hot hours in their van, stopping at dirty bathrooms and greasy fast-food places. Once she realized that negative emotions were triggered by the words "a trip across the country," she relabeled her goal to something that excited and enticed her, "the Grand Canyon." She said it made all the difference in the world.

So be specific. Not only must we label our accounts and Dream Boxes, but we must label them with something specific — not "fun" but horseback riding, not "vacation" but the Swiss Alps.

Diversify, diversify, diversify. And be specific. That's what we're talking about. If all of our money and goals are lumped together, and an unexpected expense pops up — bye-bye everything. But when we have an account in the credit union across town for Disneyland and a Dream Box for the new sofa and we send Aunt Nellie ten dollars each month to stash in case we have a big emergency — now we're talking. We're diversifying our hard-to-come-by money. We're in control, knowing our bases are covered.

When we start diversifying our money for the things we want — fun, security, travel (or to be specific, skiing, emergency money, and the Bahamas) — into various savings accounts, we begin to realize that paying ourselves first not only isn't difficult, it's energizing. With fun, security, and motivation all on our side we're on a roll. The bills, though they are still there, begin to recede into the background, and suddenly, in the shimmering light of our new awareness, stand our long-awaited goals.

You might be asking, "How can I keep track of a whole bunch of accounts? I hate paperwork. It will be so confusing."

The truth is that multiple accounts are less confusing than what most of us have been doing — and, best of all, they're fun.

For years and years I had one savings account and one checking account. When the savings statement would arrive with a balance of $91, I'd divide up the money on paper like this: "Twenty-five is for our trip to the family reunion, fifty dollars is for the table saw, and sixteen dollars is for a weekend trip to the ocean." Then the car would go in for repair. Out came the money to pay for the car, and good-bye reunion, table saw, and beach trip.

We are emotional creatures. When our one savings account statement arrives with a figure of $91, that is what registers in our brain — $91. The thought that follows might be, "Wow, that's almost a hundred dollars. Hey, I can get that new lamp that I saw on sale yesterday."

If we had separate savings accounts, we would have seen $25 as the account balance. Now our next thought might be, "Yikes, the reunion is just five months away and I don't want to miss it. With airfare, hotel, meals, and sightseeing, I'd better direct more money into this reunion account, or I won't get there."

Most of us enjoy the benefits of diversifying every day in our kitchens. We've divided our silverware into three or more sections: forks, knives, and spoons. It's not complicated, it's not confusing. In fact, it makes life easier; that's why we do it. The simple solution works every bit as well with money.

Having our money separated helps to keep us from sabotaging ourselves. We're putting a stop to withdrawing dream vacation money to pay for the latest car repair bill. Shoes aren't in the drawer with the socks, and money for the new CD player isn't mixed in with emergency money.

When the car has just been serviced, is running well, and has a full tank of gasoline, we feel confident, relaxed, and prepared to travel. That's what we're doing by diversifying our money into multiple accounts. By allocating money to cover each of our needs, we're giving ourselves the satisfaction of feeling prepared. Emergency money. Scotland money. Retirement money. Reunion money. Car money. Movie money. School money. When we have a need or a want, we take care of it. We open a separate account, specific to that goal. No more nightmares when taxes are due, no more panic when the furnace goes on the blink, no more waiting until the bills are paid off to plan and take that special trip.

Tom (the man who had saved $13,000 after a year and a half) tells his story. "I started four accounts with five dollars each and then went down a month later and opened up a couple more with five dollars. It felt good when I opened those accounts because I was organizing my money now.

"I opened up a tax-sheltered annuity account and an IRA account (not counting the other accounts I opened). I'm going to open up another account for bonus money. Then I'm going to open an account for my daughter when I don't have to pay day care anymore for her, and that will end in June. I actually have about nine accounts now. My whole future is coming together. It's a nice feeling."

Let's take stock of what happens when we diversify:

1. We've searched inside ourselves for what really motivates us and arrived at a specific goal.

2. We've taken action. We've opened separate accounts (or Dream Boxes) for each specific goal.

3. We've used the money from paying ourselves first to diversify into each of our specific goal accounts.

4. We've greatly increased our chances of actually reaching our goals. Money tucked away for a long-awaited family reunion is much less likely to be snatched to pay for the refrigerator repair bill.

5. We've established a tangible goal. We can taste, see, and feel something happening.

6. We feel relaxed and in control of our money. We've covered our bases with our various accounts (Chapter 6 shows how in depth), and we've laid the foundation for a good night's sleep.

7. We've increased the quality of our daily lives by building in anticipation, fun, motivation, and security.

8. We've created hope.

The next step will be to take your various goals and put them into an action plan. In Chapter 6, you'll learn how to create a plan for bringing your dreams to life. You'll enjoy doing it, and you'll succeed because it's a plan rooted in what you value most.

Bonnie wrote, "The other suggestion I used is to have separate savings accounts. We took few vacations before, always penny-pinching or charging up our cards. Now I have a separate savings account at my credit union where I have money taken out of every check to go to our vacation account. This summer was our first debt-free vacation. We had fun — that's a real vacation (all paid for when we got home)!

"I also have separate savings for tuition and books so I can take classes at the college. And I have an account to pay our expensive twice-yearly property taxes. We're also setting up small college accounts for our three children. And they're learning how to handle money! I never created a money plan in my life before — oh, I'd try, and get so frustrated I gave up. Now I'm finding my plan works for itself, since the items that come up 'once in a while' are taken care of by savings accounts. Another result is that I pay bills when they come now, and we don't have any more income than ever!"

How many accounts am I supposed to have?

Maybe right now you have a checking account you use for household operation, a savings account earmarked for emergencies, and a labeled container where you save all your change for an "outrageous evening on the town." If so, you've already diversified your money three ways.

Perhaps six weeks from now you get some surprise money in the form of a rebate check or money back from insurance. That bonus money may spur you on to open a car account to reduce the stress when license tags and insurance premiums are due. And if I meet you six months from now, you might say, "Hey Carol, I've got five accounts now," and three years from now, you might say, "I've got nine accounts." Once you experience the tremendous benefits of diversifying, you'll find yourself putting the concept into action as needed.

As you realize that there never seems to be enough money for such and such, you'll start a separate fund in anticipation of that event or expense. It's not a matter of deciding how many accounts to have. The challenge for each of us is to stop thinking, worrying, planning, and calculating and do it — actually put money toward our goals. With my son's room I just plain jumped in and started painting — and that's how we begin our diversified accounts. We just plain start.

If I diversify, won't I be getting less interest than if I kept the money together?

Though it seems as if we'd be losing interest by diversifying a large sum of money, let's take a closer look. If we have $500 earning 3% interest, that account would generate $15 a year. If we had $100 earning 3%, that account would earn $3 each year. Thus, five different accounts of $100 each ($500 total) would generate $3 each (or $15 altogether). We earn the same amount of interest either way. But be alert. Make certain you are not being charged a fee to save your money. The institution where you save your money should be paying *you* interest dividends for the privilege of the use of *your* money.

Where will I get the money to fund four, seven, or twelve accounts?

The first evening of a workshop Gail said, "Good grief, with what you're suggesting, I'll be ninety-seven years old when I finally get to Europe." Two thoughts seem to short-circuit us when we first entertain these new ideas: 1) "How can a few nickels and dimes ever amount to enough (for a trip to Europe before I'm ninety-seven)" and, 2) "Since I don't have any money, how will I fund all of these accounts?"

This part is always tough for me to explain because it's something that just happens. It's like standing in the rain — you get wet. My friend Brian brought his Dream Box by to show me their progress. He and his five-year-old son are saving for a seaplane ride to the San Juan Islands. Inside was a $100 bill. They had just rolled their change and had come up $3 short of an even $100. So what did they do? You guessed it. They pulled $3 out of the general fund so they'd have a crisp, new $100 bill to spur them on.

That's a great example of how we become resourceful once we're motivated. Even though Brian and his son are saving change to reach their goal, their $97 total was so close to a whopping and tantalizing $100 that $3 of non-change easily emerged to crank up the seaplane ride total. Once you set out toward your goals, you'll find all kinds of ingenious ways to get the money to make it happen. A magazine subscription will come up for renewal, and you'll weigh your priorities — more magazines? Or more money for scuba gear? Just as the longer you stand in the rain, the wetter you get, the longer you've been diversifying your money, the more ways you'll find to get additional money for your goals.

So, where does the money come from to put into these different goals? First, from our daily choices, and second, from the money games we play. (See Chapter 5.) When we drop a few coins in the hat of a street musician or panhandler, what are we saying? On some level we realize that a few coins from f people will add up to enough to help the person out. Now it's time to apply that principle to our own lives and help ourselves out.

The second week of class Gail said, "I joked about being ninety-seven years old before I'd have enough change saved for Europe, but since I've never started at all, I would have been dead! Now, at least I have a chance. I mean, I've wanted it for so long, but I really haven't done anything about getting there. I guess I just figured some day when this bill is gone, when I'm done with this, when the kids are grown, you know . . ."

Whatever your situation, start. Maybe do something as simple as slipping a little change into a sock until there's enough to go out for lunch. Choose something you'll really look forward to and stick with it. Once you've experienced reaching one goal, the success will carry you right through to the next goal and the next.

Where do I put all my accounts?

An ideal place to open the accounts for your various goals is at your local credit union. Begin by finding out if your employer is affiliated with a credit union. If so, check out what it has to offer. Next, look in the yellow pages of your phone book for credit unions in your area and be certain to ask relatives (in and out of state) about the benefits of their credit unions (membership is usually open to all family members). I'm emphasizing credit unions because their purpose is to be of service to their members, while banks are in business to make money. Both banks and credit unions are insured.

It's usually well worth the effort to find and join a credit union. The advantages of credit unions over banks are often many. Here are some benefits you may find at a credit union: higher interest on checking and savings accounts, only $5 to $50 required to open an account, lower loan rates, free or minimal monthly charges for checking accounts, no charge for savings accounts, postage-paid envelopes provided, free ATM use, store memberships, free memorial benefits, and so on. Remember to diversify where you put your money, too. We've seen savings institutions go belly up over the past years. Be sure to put your money in more than one savings institution.

People often ask if their bank or credit union will "allow" them to have more than one account. The fact is, they need our money to stay in business. Whether ten people open one account or one person opens ten accounts should make no difference. Recently a friend sent me the Boeing Credit Union newsletter. In bold letters they announced "Multiple Savings Goals — Multiple Accounts — there's no limit on the number of accounts that you can open."

Watch what you say.

Out of habit we may unconsciously be using old, familiar words that no longer accurately express what we're really feeling. Sometimes in a workshop I'll hear someone say, "I'm doing without more and more things." When I ask the group if "doing without" is what's really happening, they immediately recognize that that is not what's going on. We're no longer "doing without," we're making powerful choices. We're saying I would rather be at the ocean, I would prefer to retire early, it's my choice to buy a new stereo. Our focus has shifted. We no longer feel sorry for ourselves when we decide not to buy the item that has caught our eye. Instead, we say, "I choose to put this four seventy-five in my account for what I really want," and we purposefully keep the money separate until it lands in the proper goal account. The old attitude of "Poor me, I can't enjoy popcorn at the movies" has been replaced with "I want to eat a snack before the movie so I can put the two-fifty I would have spent on popcorn into my 'French Riviera Account.'" We're not doing *without* popcorn, we're doing *with* a first-class vacation!

How to diversify $5

When my grandmother was living, she'd slip a crisp $5 bill in my birthday card each year. As an adult I would tuck the money in my wallet and spend it on food, gasoline, or some item for the household. Writing a thank you to my grandma was always tough because I hadn't used the gift as a treat for myself. I never quite felt like writing, "Dear Grandma, Thanks for helping feed my family."

It was when I finally grasped the concept of diversifying that I began to enjoy my $5 birthday gift. I loved seeing how far I could make this money go. For example:

$2.00 for an out-to-lunch treat of a salad or sandwich
$2.00 for a new pair of earrings
$1.00 into the family fund

or

$3.50 for a movie matinee
$1.50 into the family fund

During the years I was married, we usually received an income tax refund from the IRS. While waiting for the return, I was filled with anticipation, telling others, "We're getting five hundred dollars back from the government this year!"

Finally, the $500 check would arrive. Before long I'd sit down with the bills and toss the $500 into the pile. The VISA balance might shift insignificantly, from $3,754.23 to $3,254.23. Ugh. Weeks of eager anticipation gone in an instant. And what did I do when I needed to buy a seventy-dollar replacement hose for the vacuum cleaner the next day? Charge it, of course. Since I hadn't saved any of the income tax return money, I had no choice. I had to charge. This was the self-defeating cycle I repeated for over ten years.

Then came a dramatic change. Once I caught on to diversifying, I approached the whole tax return money in a new way. During the wait for the check I would plan various ways to divide up the $500. One night it might shake down like this:

$100	Emergency account
$100	Trip to Disneyland and Grandma's house
$ 25	New carpet account
$ 30	Kids' "Now" account
$ 45	Family night out
$ 50	Christmas account
$ 50	Into the family fund to ease the squeeze
$105	New clothes

Wow, did that feel better. Spreading the money out to help meet so many needs gave me an incredible feeling of peace and control. I felt about a thousand times better than I had all those years when I watched the money vanish into the pile of bills. I found I needed to diversify the $500 on paper several different times in order to come up with a satisfying plan. I'd add or delete categories as I planned and prioritized. By the time the check arrived in the mail, I had settled on a way to diversify the money that felt extremely gratifying.

Tim wrote, "We'll get our yearly bonus next month, and we will split the money among various goals to get started on them. Only $485 out of the approximately $6,000 lump sum will go toward payment of bills. How positive is this! Hurray!"

So next time you get a windfall, whether it's money from a birthday, garage sale, rebate check, IRS return, sale of furniture or a car, inheritance, or a loan repaid, grab a piece of paper *before* you do anything with the cash, and start diversifying the money in ways that feel most satisfying to you. It works with $5, it works with $500 — diversifying your money to meet all your needs and goals is a very satisfying way to go.

THE POWER OF A LARGE LUMP SUM OF MONEY

What would most of us do if $1,000 or $25,000 landed in our hands? *Spend it.* After reading the next story and taking a peek at the following chart, we may change our minds.

About twenty-five years ago friends of mine inherited $35,000. They received the money shortly after their first child was born and did what many would do — bought a house.

But what would have happened if they had kept just $1,000 out to invest over the twenty-five years of raising their family? (Their house payments would have been only a few dollars more per month.)

The following example reflects interest rates that were available to my friends during the past twenty-five years.

		10 years	15 years	25 years	40 years
At 6%	$1,000	$1,819	$2,454	**$ 4,465**	**$ 10,954**
At 12%	$1,000	$3,300	$5,600	**$19,788**	**$118,645**

If they had put $1,000 of their inheritance money in a passbook savings account at their local bank averaging 6 percent interest over the twenty-five years, that money would have grown to $4,465 by today. But if they had taken care to get the highest possible "safe" interest over these past twenty-five years, averaging 12 percent, that one thousand would now be $19,788. That's nearly twenty thousand dollars in their pockets just for monitoring their $1,000 over the years.

But what if they had made a modest down payment on their home of $10,000 and put the remaining $25,000 of inherited money into an interest-bearing account?

		10 years	15 years	25 years	40 years
At 6%	$25,000	$45,475	$ 61,350	**$111,625**	$ 273,850
At 12%	$25,000	$82,500	$140,000	**$494,700**	**$2,966,125**

Amazing, isn't it? By placing $25,000 at the corner bank during these past twenty-five years of raising their family, they'd now have $111,625 cash. No monthly drain on the family, no pain — *more than 4 times the amount they had to start with.* How is that? It's what happens when we save a lump sum rather than spend it. And if they had made certain to get the highest bank interest possible — average 12% — they'd have nearly $500,000 today ($494,700). That $500,000 deposited today at their local bank receiving just 4% simple interest would provide my friends with a yearly interest check of $20,000 — for the rest of their lives. (When I first began saving money, I was placing $100 each month into certificate-of-deposit savings accounts that were earning 15% and 16% interest. Since I was just learning, I didn't realize the importance of signing up for a ten-year certificate that would have guaranteed that my money would earn 15% and 16% interest for the next ten years. I did lock my money in for two and a half years though!)

Two years ago when I had to stop putting money into my tax-sheltered annuity, it totaled $15,027.00. This month's statement reveals a new balance of $17,593.70. That's an increase of $2,566. This account has been growing at the rate of $100 a month — all on its own!

Marlow, a real estate agent, wrote, "I am constantly running into people who have just sold a home, have a huge chunk of money, and are ready to put the whole sum into a new house. I always knew this was folly but floundered when I attempted to point out why — I just couldn't seem to come up with enough good reasons. Now, with the information I learned in your workshop and the charts you have provided, I'm able to help people keep from making a serious financial mistake."

SUMMARY

Diversifying our money is one of the best ways I know for making life lots more fun and reaching our goals at the same time. We're relaxed knowing we're prepared for emergencies, and we're energized and filled with anticipation as we experience our dreams and goals coming true.

Remember how important it is to be specific. When we say we're "saving money" or "saving for vacation," the idea is vague and intangible, hardly something to get worked up about. But when we turn the plain word "vacation" into Aspen, Bermuda, Greece, Africa, or New Zealand — suddenly we come alive. We have a reason to save and we suddenly want to gather all the money we can find.

The moment money is placed in an interest-bearing account, it begins to grow and multiply — all on its own. Before you *spend* a large sum of money, ask yourself, "How long would it take me to accumulate this much again? How much interest earnings will I lose on the lump sum over the years if I spend the money instead of saving it?" For most of us lump sums of money are hard to come by. If a chunk of money lands in your hands, *hold on to it.*

FIVE

Myths, Money Games, and More

Tell them to enjoy it while they can, not like
us. When you're in your eighties you have the
money but can't go.
— Katherine Keeffe Johnson

I'M calling a "myth" those things we *assume* to be true — though there really is no written rule or standard. For example, a myth I lived by for years was that people have one savings account. It never occurred to me to open multiple savings accounts. I assumed everyone had one checking and one savings account.

MYTHS

I hope that by exploring the following myths you'll begin questioning other patterns in your life and discovering where you've been operating out of "assumptions." I invite you to reconsider your thoughts, feelings, and opinions about these and all other myths in your life and see if you might come up with choices you've never considered before. (I remember the time I placed a chest of drawers out in the entryway of the house. It was tough to do because the myth I had always operated from was that dressers belong in the bedroom. But the chest looked good there and solved a space problem.)

Take time to notice for yourself. Are myths ruling you, or are you carefully considering what you value most in life and then choosing to act? (Our challenge is to keep turning over stones — to keep searching beyond the assumption for what is best for us.) We all deserve quality and satisfaction in life, but it won't just happen, we have to choose it.

Myth #1: You should own your own home

Once I became an adult, I heard it from practically everywhere, "When are you going to buy a house? Owning a home is the best investment you will ever make. You're not going to throw your money away renting, are you?" I don't remember discussions about the pros and cons of buying or renting. It was *assumed* that buying is what you do. The entire myth goes like this: "You grow up, get a good job, marry, buy a house, and have kids." There was never a question about whether to own my own home; the message was always *when* was I going to buy?

So much of the input we get in our lives is like this. We're fed the party line, and we begin to behave as if the party line is the only way. Unfortunately, once we're conditioned, we're not likely to question what we've learned. "The idea of challenging preconceptions like 'I must own a home' was revolutionary to me and incredibly freeing," said Marina.

The way the economy and society are today, and given our individuality, we can't assume that buying a home is the "right" way to go. I remember Marty speaking up at a workshop, "My husband and I only owned our house for six months before we sold it. We were both working long hours, fighting constantly, and never had any time to just relax with our infant son. We thought we had bought the house for him, but finally realized there was no time or energy for him anymore. Our whole life revolved around how to get enough money to make the house payment and still live." How many times is the quality of family life ruined because of the pressure to come up with a huge house payment (not to mention money for a new roof, plumbing problems, yard work, pest control, furnace repair, taxes)?

Whether it's best to own or rent is a question to ask ourselves throughout our lives. As our needs change, so does the kind of housing we need. We want to carefully figure out which is best for us, based on our own lifestyle, finances, and values. At first, many people who took my money workshop didn't think buying was even remotely possible in their financial situation. When I talked with Mary, age fifty-six years, two years later, here's what she said. "Before I took your workshop I felt indebted to my bills and I felt trapped. Life looked pretty bleak. You made a point that had an impact on me when you asked, 'What is your dream? If it's important to have a house, then that's okay, focus on that. If it's important to travel and not spend as much on housing, then focus on that. Get in touch with what is really important to you.' I was living in the basement of a nice home in a nice area, but it wasn't someplace that I wanted to stay the rest of my life. I didn't even consider buying. At the time I thought, 'If you don't have two incomes, you can't do it in this city. I'm doomed to renting.' That's how the scene looked at the time.

"By accident I was conversing with someone and saying, 'Oh, I wish I could buy a place of my own, but I just can't do it.' And they said they had seen a really nice town house that was a HUD (federal Department of Housing and Urban Development) home. It seemed feasible. I started looking around, set a goal, and started saving. I learned to take my paycheck and pay myself and *then* write checks out for the bills. What's left is what I have to live on. Pretty soon I was at about a thousand dollars and I said, 'This is really a thrill!'

"In a year and a half, I have saved about ten thousand dollars. I'll be moving into my condominium the nineteenth of this month. I'm fifty-six years old, and when I came here life looked so bleak and hopeless. Even when I was at your class two years ago, achieving that goal felt almost impossible. It was not easy, I'll be the first to say that. But to see that my goal could be realized was the hope. And I didn't scrimp. I probably could have saved more, but I have a thing about cash. If I bought something, I paid cash."

Before we run out and invest tens of thousands into buying a home or before we dismiss the idea that we "never can own," we need to keep asking ourselves, "What kind of housing will best suit my/our needs at this point in life?"

Valerie spoke up. "A coworker of mine and his wife withdrew $10,000 from their IRA [retirement account] to use as a down payment on a house. I've seen him go from fun weekend ski trips to being completely stressed out. Every payday it's just worse and worse — waiting for the check, worrying about estimated taxes and how to make the mortgage payment. He went from paying $450 a month for rent to having a mortgage payment of over $1200 a month, plus two car payments, plus a baby. I look at him and think, 'I'm glad I didn't do it that way.'" It's a sad situation that's all too common: the quality of life for three people is being eroded away — all because of a house payment.

I invite you to evaluate carefully your emotional and financial housing needs — now, and throughout your life. A friend mentioned to me today that he'll be working harder and longer in hopes of holding on to his house after his divorce. My heart felt heavy as he focused on longer hours and increased stress — all for the sake of being a homeowner — at a time in his life when he desperately needs to ease his emotional and financial pressures.

Karren came to the second money class bursting with the news that she had rented an apartment for $200 a month less than she had planned — all because of our discussion. Before class she searched the ads in the price range she thought she could afford based on her salary. After class she searched for apartments based on the quality of life she really wanted. Not only would Karren have $200 more a month (or $2,400 a year!) to save and diversify for her goals, she also said, "My apartment is a bit smaller than my last but it has a breathtaking, one-hundred-and-eighty-degree view of the water!"

Over and over again I hear couples say, "I wish one of us could be home with our children, but we both have to work just to get by." Most often this is a myth rather than a fact. Years ago I read that the first ten thousand dollars plus that is earned by the second working parent goes to pay for child care, transportation, work clothes, higher food bills (packaged meals, expensive convenience foods, and eating out more frequently because of anxiety and fatigue), higher medical bills due to increased stress, and so on. Too often we think we're bringing in more money, when, in fact, we're creating more bills plus greater stress and loss of relaxed family time.

T. J. and her husband live consciously for what they value most. "John and I have talked and talked about how much money we need as a family to be comfortable. John has been a home daddy for almost two years, and we home-school our two daughters. I work four evening shifts a week (thirty-two hours) as a nurse, and at this point we feel rich!"

What do *you* really want? To work four days a week? To be home with your children? To have more time to relax? To be free of house maintenance responsibilities? To have a space of your own? Once you know what really matters to you, then you can search for a way to make it happen. For myself, I have a tremendous inner feeling of satisfaction knowing I have made being home with my children a priority.

There are so many issues when it comes to the pros and cons of owning or renting. Too often the professional advice we're given is based on long-term gain. This approach may look impressive on paper, but it ignores the emotional needs that make life satisfying and enjoyable *today*. Paying extra or double on house payments is a good example of this. Certainly paying more will get the home paid off sooner and possibly reduce the interest payments by tens of thousands, but what does it do to the quality of life in the meantime? For myself, I need money for today. My highest priority right now is having the resources to provide adequately for myself and the needs of my two teenage sons, not getting my house paid off faster.

Here's what Patti decided upon questioning her paper plan. "We have reevaluated paying extra principal payments on our house. We will be saving and diversifying our money instead in order to enjoy life more now. We're stopping to smell the roses before the winter in our life comes and the roses are all gone."

Our challenge is to question the path we're on. Just because a decision we made felt or seemed right when we started doesn't mean it's still best for us today. So often we think that because we've made a certain choice, we must stick with it. Not true. The most rewarding choice in the short and long run may be to change our minds.

Myth #2: People retire at age sixty-five

Why do most people work full-time to age sixty-five or older? Because they don't have enough money to retire sooner. The fact is, retirement has nothing to do with age. Retirement has to do with financial independence — having the money to choose where, when, and whether to work at all.

This was an incredible realization for me — that *I* choose my age of "retirement." (By "retired," I simply mean having the money to choose whether to work or not.) We each have places to go, things to do, peoples' lives to touch, passions to pursue — all of which we could do freely if only we didn't have to work every day just to get by. So what is the age of retirement? Whatever age we choose. All we need to do is put away the money that will buy us the freedom of choice.

Myth #3: Every family owns two cars

The bottom line when it comes to cars is that they are a means of getting us from here to there. However, advertising has roped many of us into believing that the engine and metal sitting outside our door reflect who we are. Self-image, status, pride, glamour, prestige, power, importance have all become entangled in getting us transported from home to the grocery store. It helps to be aware of this phenomenon so we can make certain we're choosing based on what we really want and not on what we feel we should do to get approval from others.

In a workshop I ask people how they could have arrived if they didn't have access to a car. In a local Seattle workshop, most people readily mention walking, riding a bike, hitching a ride, and taking a city bus. They seldom mention the most likely means for this area — taxi, car pool, and rental car.

"Rent a car? Take a taxi? I can't afford it," is what I usually hear. Not long after taking the money workshop, Noni sent me a note saying, "I'm wondering if it's worth calling my debtors and asking for a one-month extension. I've been fearful of that, but it would help us so much. I have not even paid us first because there's no extra money at all."

Their financial condition sounded pretty desperate. A call to Noni revealed *two* new-car payments, one for $378 and the other for $319. It's incredible. Almost $700 out the window each month! Is it any wonder there's no money left for food and light bulbs — much less paying themselves first?

What surprises me even more than seeing the ways people become overextended is the thinking that keeps us in the trap. As I was talking with Noni, she reasoned that to sell her car now was senseless because there were only fourteen months of payments left. Only? Immediately I calculated that $378 \times 14 = \$5{,}292$ worth of payments left — and that's only for the one car! It's hard to imagine a family struggling for fourteen more months all because of car payments. (After this story I love my 1981, $2,200 economy car more than ever.) If Noni chose to sell her car, she could buy an excellent used car, probably have cash left in her pocket, and have $378 *more* in the family account every month for the next fourteen months. What would you choose?

What's curious is that so many of us think we "can't afford" a taxi or rental car. How many times could Noni rent a used car or take a cab during the month before she'd even come close to the price of her car payment — not to mention the cost of license tags, insurance, tires, and repair. (I pay $12 a day when I rent a used car.)

Judy said, "I had been without a car for about a year and

got along fine. If I needed to go someplace on the weekend, I would rent a car. I chose to put it on my American Express card because it would cover the liability if something happened, and I would get an itemized bill. My bill for that entire year was three hundred and eighty-three dollars for rental of cars.

"Then my daughter turned sixteen and wanted a car because all her friends had one. When she got a second job, I gave in. The day I picked up the car I had to get new license tags, and that was a hundred dollars. Because she was under eighteen, the insurance cost about six hundred dollars (even though she had good grades). Just picking up that car, I probably laid out eight hundred dollars — not including what I was going to be spending for maintenance, gas, and all that other stuff. If I hadn't gone through it, I would not have believed it. Not only was it a lot cheaper not to own a car, I planned my life better. When I wanted to go shopping, I'd rent a car or walk to the grocery store and take a cab back home. My life was much more pleasurable. I had money to do other things, and now it was being tied up by this car, and I was resenting it a lot."

I actually consider myself lucky that we had only one car for the first eighteen years of my marriage. (At that point my parents gave us their car when they bought a newer model.) Why was I lucky? Because I had the opportunity to experience the freedom of *not* having a car at my disposal. If my children were sick, I'd call a cab for a ride to the clinic. I never was stuck. In a squeeze my wonderful neighbors would let me borrow their car or truck. There was always a way to get where I needed to go. Not having a car in the driveway left me feeling free to stay home and relax with my kids. So many people exclaim, "Oh no! I couldn't *live* without my car." That's often because they have no idea of the freedom they'd experience. If you run out of stamps or juice, you don't use your precious time, energy, and gasoline to drive and pick up just one item. You relax and plan. You know you're going to rent a car on Wednesday, and that's when you'll do your errands. Think about times you've been without a ride or your car's been in the shop. Once you resigned yourself to being home, you most likely felt a taste of freedom.

"My awareness was raised by your discussion of the actual cost of having a [second] car and other conveniences," said Ellen. "The cost of owning and operating a car today is staggering (not to mention the toll they are taking on the environment)." More often than not, cars are a major source of tension in our lives. The cost of owning and maintaining a car drains money that could have gone for necessities and fun, and too often we pack our days by going, going, going from here to there and back again just because we can. Ellen continued, "Now I really think about whether that little luxury is worth the continuing expensive maintenance."

For this next week try standing back and observing yourself. What do you notice? Are you carefully planning and making conscious choices about how you spend your time, energy, and money for transportation?

Myth #4: This is my lot in life. I'll always be trying to make ends meet

For years I felt divided inside. Part of my brain said, "Carol, you live in the United States of America. You can be whoever you want to be. You can do whatever you want to do. You can own your own business; you can run for president of the United States. Part of me felt open to unlimited possibilities, and the other part of me was saying, "Poor me, this is my lot in life. I'll always be trying to make ends meet." What about you? What's going on in your mind? Has part of you given up? Or are you determined that you are in charge of your money and your life and can make it what you want it to be?

MONEY GAMES: FINDING MONEY FOR YOUR DREAMS – AS EASY AS PLAYING A GAME

You've probably been wondering where you're going to get the money to fund all your goals. Following are twenty-five money games to get you going. Each game provides the incentive of a fun or creative way to uncover money for your goals. Like Lynn, if you give some of these games a try, you, too, will be saying, "Money is coming my way now."

1. ¢hange Game. This is by far the most popular and most successful game. Refer to page 15 in Chapter 1 for a full discussion of the ¢hange Game.

2. Found Money or Extra Money Game. I finally came up with the idea for this game when I was desperately trying to figure out a way to get my kids to Disneyland while they were still children. I remember opening a Disneyland account with $35 of Christmas money. Nine months later the account still had about $35 in it (a bit more with the interest). I was frustrated. I couldn't see any way to squeeze more money out of our monthly income. Finally I began snatching up all "found money" and funneling it into this account. "Found" or "extra" money was cash received from birthday or holiday gifts, rebate checks, refunds, coupons, gifts, machine returns, recycling, store returns, bottle returns, and any other unexpected money that came my way. Nine months after starting the Found Money game, we packed up the car and headed for Disneyland.

3. The Choice Game. This game came about as soon as I realized that just $3 saved a day becomes $1,095 in a year. What began to happen is that I'd see a small item in the store (earrings, a knickknack, toy for the kids, snack item) that in the past I would have bought without thinking. Now, I'd see the item as ONE THOUSAND DOLLARS!

This new awareness led me to the Choice Game. Now when I'm tempted by a small, inconsequential item, I ask myself, "Would I rather have the item or would I rather put that money in my Dream Box and reach my goal sooner?" What's wonderful is that there's no guilt or feeling of being deprived if I pass up the item — in fact, it's fun and exciting to consciously make the empowering choice to take the money home to my Dream Box for something I really want.

Matt said that three and a half years ago he gave up buying his lunch (about $4 a day) to help family finances. He was angry and felt cheated because there had been no difference in the amount of money they had nor in the quality of their lives as a result of his sacrifice. He sat in class and calculated three and a half years of sack lunches and realized that $4 times 5 days in the week times 50 weeks in the year was $3,500! Matt made the choice to pack his lunch but forgot to redirect the money. No money is saved unless we actually *save* it. The key to our success is in how we feel. In our new feel-great-about-money approach we're saying good-bye to the negative emotions of "giving up" and "doing without" and re-warding ourselves with a payoff for our new choices.

4. Cash Machine or ATM Game. Patricia said she used to stop at the ATM every Friday night and withdraw $20 to spend with her friends. Now, she continues to withdraw $20 from the ATM, but her goal is to have as much money left as possible at the end of the evening to put in her Dream Box.

5. Working Overtime for a Goal. What a difference in our energy and attitude when we know our overtime pay will fund our goals instead of our bills!

6. Extra Work or Money from Hobbies for Our Goals. Once you start listing your dreams and goals, you're going to want to figure out more and more ways to make them happen. I took a paper route delivering the local community news every Wednesday morning for the money to buy my love seat. What way(s) might you come up with to create some extra income to fund your goals?

7. Checkbook Subtracting Game. This idea is fun to do, can add up to a lot, and simplifies record keeping when you're out and about. When you write a check at the grocery store for $65.17, enter the amount in your check register as you've always done. For example:

Check No.	Date	Item	Check Amount	Balance
1756	2/26	Favorite Grocery Store	**$65.17**	$123.00
				−66.00

But when you subtract, round the amount up to the next dollar, from $65.17 to $66.00 (see example). This makes subtracting easy, and each time you write a check, you're sneaking a little money away. Then, when you actually sit down to balance the checkbook, you can subtract the "real" amounts. The extra money saved is yours for your goal.

8. Checkbook Change Game. Before you write a check to make a purchase, round up the amount to the next dollar. For example, if the item you are buying costs $43.21, you would write the check for $44.00. The cashier will hand you 79¢ in change. Take the money home and make sure it gets into your Dream Box.

9. Two Checking Accounts Game. This is one of the all-time great games for those who hate to reconcile their checkbook with the bank statement. Dave explained how he does it. "I operate exclusively out of one checking account for three months, then I stop using that account altogether so all the checks I've written can clear the bank and I'll know how much money I have in that account. Meanwhile, I use my other account for the next three months." Clever. This approach not only eliminates the anguish and guilt of not balancing the checkbook, it also provides a new source of revenue for our goals because we'll have to keep extra money in the account to prevent overdraft charges. At the end of three months, when the account balances out, all the "extra" money built up can be transferred directly into one of our goals.

10. Co-signature Account Game. One time when I was out of town visiting my youngest sister, Shari, she decided she would like some help saving money. We sat together at the bank and asked to open a co-signature savings account. The young teller happily pulled out the necessary paperwork and started asking questions. When I told her my address, three hundred miles away, a look of alarm replaced her smile and she said to my sister, "Oh, you don't want a co-signature account because you won't be able to withdraw money without your sister's signature." With a huge smile on her face my sister nodded. "I know." This game engages the help of a friend or relative to help us reach our goals.

11. Canadian Money Game. Since we live fairly near the Canadian border, we frequently find Canadian coins in our change. We enjoy saving them for "fun money" when we visit British Columbia.

12. Coupon Game. Saving coupons, hauling them around, and trying to remember to cash them in was always too much hassle for me. Besides, I've never been able to get all worked up over reducing my $87.92 grocery bill to $87.42 with a couple of 25¢ coupons. But when there's something I really want and the cash back from coupons is the source to fund the goal, suddenly I'm motivated to carry those little coupons all the way to the register in exchange for cash in my hand for my goal. Most cashiers are happy to give cash in exchange for the coupon rather than merely subtracting the amount from the bill (assuming you've bought the corresponding product). But if it seems to be a problem, go ahead and pay the cashier first and then hand over the coupon. You'll automatically be given cash you can take home to stash away for your goal.

13. Loan Account Game. Sometimes when a loan is established, a savings account is opened to facilitate transaction of payments. Now, when we deposit the money to cover the loan payment, we include a few extra dollars. The added money accumulates with interest during the span of the loan — one more way to sneak out a bit of money to reach a goal.

14. The Percentage Game. Using percentages to help diversify our money is a fun and very satisfying way to go. Rather than depositing a certain dollar amount toward a goal each month, save a percentage. For example, you might decide to put 60% of all "found" money toward your vacation account and 40% toward your emergency fund. Or, instead of $20 a month deposited into a new furniture account, it could be 1% of every paycheck. Using percentage amounts is a very effective and satisfying solution for anyone who is self-employed, on commission, or working at a seasonal job. Play with the percentage idea, and see what creative ideas you come up with to help you attain your goals.

15. New Choice Game. Keep your eyes open for every opportunity to make a new choice with your money. If it's time to renew a magazine or club membership, you may decide you'd rather direct that money toward your goals. It's your choice.

16. Put It In, Take It Out Game. My son came up with this next game. "Go ahead and shop as usual," he says, "gathering all the items you'd ordinarily buy. But before you head to the register to pay, take a minute to check over your selection. If there are any items you decide you don't really want, put them back, but *right then* take the exact amount you would have spent and put it in your pocket to take home as cash for your dreams."

17. Diversify Your Change Game. You guessed it. Quarters for one goal, nickels for another, dimes and pennies for a third and fourth — or any combination you choose.

18. Laundry Game. When you play this game your goal is funded by the money you find in pockets while sorting the laundry. After her son was born, one woman began slipping all the "pocket money" she found into an umbrella that sat near the washing machine. On his wedding day she presented her son with the cash she had dropped in the umbrella throughout his life.

19. Friendly Competition. Now that you're zeroing in on your goals, you may want to increase your efficiency and incentive by competing with a coworker or friend. Knowing that each payday you're going to "compare progress" may spur you both on to arrive at your goals even sooner.

20. Centrally Locating Your Dream Box. You might be surprised how willing relatives and friends are to part with their change. Make it easy for them to help you reach your goal by leaving your labeled Dream Box sitting out in a conspicuous spot. (Remember that change adds up fast — a small paper roll of quarters equals $10. Protect yourself by rolling the money regularly and adding it to your account to earn interest.)

21. Forming a Good Habit (or Extinguishing a Bad Habit). This game is a chance to pat yourself on the back. Perhaps you're giving up swearing, smoking, or drinking. Each time you choose an alternative, reward yourself (for example, drop in a quarter for your goal). Or, if you're adopting more healthful behaviors, such as walking twenty minutes a day or eating more vegetables, pat yourself on the back by depositing small change for each success. In class one time Debbie said, "People have told me I should reward myself with new clothes for giving up smoking, but where was I supposed to get the money to celebrate with? Now I know!"

22. Pennies for Investment. Years ago the evening news showed a man and woman walking up to a bank with a red wagon in tow. They were pulling over $2,000 worth of pennies for use as a down payment on a home. Laura suggested that over the next few years while we're building our security funds and becoming in control of our money, it's a great time to save all our pennies for investing. Pennies saved over the years are perfect for our first shot at "gambling" in the stock market. (Even if we lost the money, we probably wouldn't lose any sleep.)

23. The Three-Day Waiting Game. Sometimes when I'm at a store, I just have to have a certain item. To check whether I've made a wise choice or merely an impulsive buy,

I leave the item in the sack when I get home and place it where I'll notice it as I walk about the house. Before long something happens. Either I'm glad I bought the item and it comes out of the sack, or, as the days go by, I realize that what I really need is the cash, and I return the item.

Another way to use the Three-Day Waiting game occurs when I see a sale in the newspaper. Instead of jumping in the car and running out to shop, I've learned to tack the ad on the refrigerator and wait. Usually by the third day I've realized this item is not my top priority, and I drop the ad in the recycling sack.

24. Matching Funds Game. The concept of matching funds can be used in as many creative ways as you can come up with. Mary Ann said, "I decided my luxury was a housekeeper, and if I could afford x amount of dollars for this, then I should be able to match at least the same amount for savings. It's taken me a period of about six months to get to where I'm matching the exact amount that I pay my housekeeper per month — but I did it."

Another way to "match" is with your children. I remember when my son had to have the latest game that "all" the other kids were playing. Not impressed with the game or the cost (almost $100), I told him I wouldn't be buying it for him. Finally, we struck a deal. If he earned half the money, I'd match for the balance. It was a tremendous incentive, and he had the game in no time.

25. Doubling Day. A dad attending one of my money workshops shared this game. At some unpredictable point in the month he announces to his children, "Today is doubling day." The kids then show him how much money they have saved, and he doubles the amount. What a great incentive for kids to save their money.

26. The Best Game of All. Making sure your hard-to-come-by-money is being carefully and consciously directed toward what you value most.

Reminder. ¢hange adds up fast. A peanut can or mayonnaise jar can easily hold one hundred dollars or more. You'll want to count and roll your change every few weeks to get the boost of the new total, to feel the dream coming true, and to get the money to the credit union, where it may be safer than at home and can be earning interest.

BUYING TIPS

✦ **How many hours?** Before we spend our money, we may want to ask ourselves, "How many hours did I spend working in order to make enough money to pay for this?" Or, to put it another way, "Would I work a half day (or however much time) if this item were my reward in the end?"

✦ **Be carefree.** From time to time go on an outing with no money, no checks, and no credit cards. Notice all the thoughts and feelings that come up for you. It may be an eye-opening experience. Since you can't buy anything, you may feel "free" to browse, relax, and perhaps be aware of people, places, and items you've never noticed before.

✦ **Don't be in a hurry.** Often, when we realize we're out of batteries, need a light bulb, or are low on groceries, we head for the store without thinking. A great way to reduce stress and keep more money in your pocket is to slow down and *plan* errands. A guideline might be to have at least three errands or a minimum of five items to buy at the store before going out. (Our wise choices enhance our lives; we're spending more time stopping to smell the flowers.)

✦ **Be creative.** Usually we wait until circumstances force us to be creative (such as arriving at a picnic with no silverware, or having to prepare a dinner during a power outage). Now, we can *choose* to be creative. Rather than taking the time and money to buy every little convenience item, we can choose to free up time and money for what we really want. For example, perhaps you decide your habit of buying fabric softener for the laundry is a luxury, so you take that money and apply it toward a goal instead.

✦ **Shop from sale to sale.** The goal is to buy enough of an item when it's on sale to last until it's on sale again. At first it seems we won't be able to afford to do this. It is quite doable, though, because this week we buy eight cans of frozen orange juice but no olives or tomato sauce. Next week tomato sauce is on sale and we stock up on enough to last about six weeks or until the next sale. Instead of buying a little bit of everything at high prices, we buy enough of the sale items we need to last us until the next sale. The benefit? By buying on sale we can reduce our food bill up to 30%. In other words, a $340 monthly food bill could be reduced to $238 — that means an extra $102 available for funding goals and other needs.

✦ **You're in charge when you're buying.** Remember, when you're buying (particularly a big-ticket item like furniture or appliances), *you* have the power because the salesperson and the store want your business. Often we can get 10% to 20% off the ticket price by offering to buy it now, with cash. If they're not interested in reducing the price of the item, be sure to ask what other merchandise or benefits they'll "throw in" with the purchase (for example, a carrying case and software when buying computers). Many stores offer "ninety days the same as cash" as a payment option. (If you pay in full within three months, ninety days, there are no interest charges.)

Negotiate. Yesterday I saw a beautiful picture frame on sale, but the only one left was the one on display and it had a few minor scratches. I asked the clerk to consult the manager for an additional $3 off the sale price. Done. Remember, the person with the money has the power — and that person is *you.*

✦ **Does it have to be new?** Often we can get much more than we ever dreamed we could afford by purchasing secondhand. Have you discovered the secondhand sports and music stores? How about auctions, newspaper ads, and garage sales? What options do you have to get the most for your money?

✦ **It's the thought that counts.** Birthdays, holidays, anniversaries, weddings — it's so easy to forget that these are love celebrations and that it's the thought that counts (not the size or price of the gift). Before shopping it's a great exercise to pause and make sure we're operating from the inside. Are we giving from the heart? Are we sure the cost and the number of gifts we're choosing to give don't hurt ourselves or our family's needs? Are we operating out of guilt or giving to prove something or impress someone? Hopefully, we're reminding ourselves that gifts are a simple gesture of love and caring. (If what we're giving isn't coming from love and caring, perhaps it's really not a gift.)

✦ **A gift idea.** I heard that one young man's girlfriend celebrated her birthday the day after the money workshop. He bought her one of each of her favorite flowers, a rose and an orchid, and gave her five dollars to open a new account!

STARTING YOUR OWN IRA ACCOUNTS PUTS YOU IN CHARGE

An IRA (Individual Retirement Account) is a tremendous way to save. IRAs were created to give the everyday person with an everyday paycheck the opportunity and the incentive to save money. An IRA is a retirement account you are in control of. Unlike pension and social security money, this is money you put away for yourself — you're the one in charge.

Basically, an IRA is a savings account with several added benefits. Here are three excellent reasons to open an IRA as soon as possible: 1) You don't have to pay tax on the interest money generated by your IRA. (This becomes a significant advantage as your IRA builds and is generating thousands of dollars in interest.) 2) IRAs receive higher interest than regular savings accounts because the money will probably remain in savings for some time. 3) Depending on your income, the money you deposit in your IRA may reduce your taxable income.

An IRA can be opened with as little as $25. If that's all you deposit in your account, you'll still benefit from the advantages mentioned above. As long as you have earned money sometime during the calendar year, you may deposit up to $2,000 of that earned income into an IRA. Keep in mind the magic of compound interest. Take a moment right now to turn to the charts on pages 194–197. If you begin soon to put $10 or $20 from each paycheck into your own IRA account, your money will double, quadruple, and more, over time. I encourage you to have as one of your goals getting your own IRA started within the next year. Remember, once you've got it started, it will be growing and compounding on its own and it's all your money.

Begin with small, regular monthly deposits to your IRA and raise the ante as you go. Set your sights for an eventual $167 monthly IRA deposit and you will have reached the $2,000 maximum yearly deposit.

You may be wondering, "But what if I want to retire before age fifty-nine and a half" (the age at which you can withdraw money from your IRA without a 10% penalty). Because of the benefits listed above, even with early withdrawal of some of the funds, an IRA is still one of the best investments you can make. It's important to understand that if you withdraw IRA money before age fifty-nine and a half, you pay a penalty only on the amount you actually withdraw, not on the entire amount in the account.

Remember to diversify your IRA money. This is your security money. Make certain it's not all at one institution. You have until April 15 (income tax due date) to open an IRA for the previous tax year. An IRA is probably the best way for the average American to accumulate a sizable amount of money without having to pay tax on the interest earned. Best of all, unlike pension or social security money, *you* are in control of your own IRA money.

INSURANCE TIPS

Insurance is a huge topic. My goal is simply to remind you to take a close, educated look at your needs and coverage for your medical, disability, dental, car, home, and life insurance policies.

Our needs are always changing. Each year at policy renewal time take a few minutes to reevaluate your own needs. If you injured your back or needed daily medication and physical therapy, would your medical policy provide adequate coverage? (Remember, the big print giveth and the small print taketh away.) Are your household belongings (furniture, jewelry, appliances, clothing) adequately covered with renters insurance or homeowner insurance? If so, have you specified *replacement* value in the event that something is stolen or destroyed or are you insured only for current (used) value? How about life insurance? Do you even need it? (Remember, it's actually death insurance — money that goes to someone else only after you die.)

Does your employer provide dental or vision insurance, and are you taking advantage of the benefits? Have you telephoned and compared rates on car insurance to take advantage of safe-driver prices and other benefits? Particularly if you are self-employed, have you asked yourself, "Do I have adequate disability insurance in the event I couldn't work?"

Probably the best way to do your shopping for insurance is on the telephone. When you're asking for information and you've run out of questions, pose this one: "What haven't I asked you that I might want to know?"

SUMMARY

Remember to question your assumptions. It may be that you are operating on assumptions that are myths. Now is a great time to reevaluate habits and patterns. On close inspection you may discover choices you never realized you had.

The chapter you've just read is one you may want to refer back to as your money plan grows and expands. Let these ideas be springboards for you. It's a sure thing you'll invent your own ingenious ways to harvest money to feed your dreams.

SIX

Planning for Your Happiness — Today and Tomorrow

Obstacles are those frightful things you see when you take your eyes off your goals.
— Henry Ford

I'VE come to realize that the act of making plans is a formidable fear for many of us. Often, before we can even entertain a plan, our mind constructs an elaborate set of logical reasons why it will never work out, when all along, the real reason we don't proceed might be that we are afraid. Here's an example. The idea of a vacation in the Caribbean sounds inviting — crystal-clear waters for awe-inspiring snorkeling, lazy days in the soothing sun, adventure, good food, fun. Finally a good buddy asks us one day, "When are you going to stop talking and go?" Immediately our mind whips out a long list of obstacles: "Oh, it's not the right time just now and besides I've used up my vacation time and it's probably not all it's cracked up to be and it's sure to cost way more than I should spend on a vacation and I need to put a new roof on the house in the next year and . . ."

Beneath this long list of can'ts we will most often find a fear — and this fear could be any one of a number of things. It might be fear of disappointment. What if we made all the plans to go and something happened at the last minute that caused us to cancel the trip? (Airline strike, illness, problems at work.) Many of us have been so disappointed in our lives by parents, relatives, the weather, friends, bosses, that we protect ourselves to the extent that we won't even make plans. Other fears might be our appearance, our weight, our lack of "proper" Caribbean vacation clothes. Or maybe it's our fear of airplanes, boats, leaving the country, being in new places, being far away from family doctors, and so on.

My point? If you find yourself resisting the idea of making a plan for yourself — STOP and ask yourself why? What's blocking you from setting in place a plan that will help you realize your dreams and give you the peaceful feeling of being in control of your money? Either stop and correct what is interfering with your progress, or plow right on through the fear and start your plan anyway, as Mary did. "Before we could leave your workshop we had to submit a plan. I was grateful for that. Creating a plan for myself forced me to really take a look and not escape. It's like, 'Gee, I think I could start saving a little bit.' And so I made that decision and I stuck with it. I had money taken out from my paycheck for savings and I took a small amount, like twenty-five dollars or something like that, a pay period."

In order to succeed, your money plan has to be fun and it has to be what you want. The first step is to zero in on what motivates you the most. For Tony, it was a red mountain bike; for Mary, her hiking boots; for Elaine, age fifty-seven, it was a retirement fund; and for Kay and Bob it was a trip to Scotland. Over the years you will continue to revise and expand your money plan until it becomes comprehensive. To start with, however, it must be so easy and motivating that you're certain to succeed.

The question to ask yourself is, "What would improve the quality of my daily life? The answer might be money to hire a child care provider so you can get some needed time alone, money for a guilt-free clothing item, or a weekend getaway for rest and relaxation. As you go about the day, reflect on what your first goal will be. Perhaps, like Leslie blinded by her $7,000 MasterCard debt, you're having difficulty remembering what it is you really long for.

For most of us there are two things that would make a big difference in the quality of our lives: (1) having the deeply satisfying feeling of knowing we're directing money toward making our dreams come true, and (2) having the secure feeling of knowing money is available for today's emergencies as well as tomorrow's needs.

If you were thinking that eliminating a bill would make a significant difference in the quality of your life, *watch out.* It's only a diversionary tactic of the mind. Of course things would be better if the bills were more under control or gone altogether. But eliminating a bill creates only a temporary feeling of relief compared with the deep and lasting feelings of power and security that money in hand creates. The availability of money means choices, and choices mean control. Lack of bills will never compare to the potency of having choices (money).

To help get your mind off the bills, let's pretend your wish comes true — you have no bills. Now what? What's still missing? What would you like to be anticipating that would give a boost to your days? How about planning and saving for a fun item or outing? Or are fun and extravagance the daily fare and what you're longing for is the security of your own money in hand?

Here's what Ellen did to help herself sort out what excited her the most for right now. "I made a list of things I would like to do — little goals, and then some bigger ones. I brainstormed about what goals I would like and then I chose one — a weekend away." Great idea. Write down every single idea that pops into your head. Don't edit yourself. Allow every idea to flow. After a few days of adding to your list, you'll probably find that one or two goals attract you a bit more than the others. Listen to that attraction and don't analyze it. The goal you're thinking about might be frivolous or practical. *Trust yourself.* If it excites you to think about it, go with it.

When I'm giving a workshop and I'm walking around helping people design a plan, I'm amazed at how much negativity creeps into their plans. Just because I've talked about having money saved for an emergency or dollars socked away for car repairs, some people feel they should include those on their first plan. Wrong. The only goals written on your first plan are the ones that highly motivate you, goals that keep you chomping at the bit.

There aren't good plans, bad plans, right plans, or wrong plans — there is only *your* plan for making your dreams come true. In Mary's story she talks about needing to buy a home for herself in order to feel secure as she approaches retirement. For Mary, owning her own place was an important and highly motivating goal. Someone else might reject the idea of home ownership, not wanting to be tied down in retirement to home maintenance and taxes — it might be the last thing they want. Your task is to decide what *you* want.

Discerning what really motivates you right now in your life is probably both the trickiest and the most critical part of designing a successful plan. Take the time to focus and carefully discriminate between what you really want and what you think you should do. It's time to throw out the agendas of others and *trust your own inner wisdom.*

Following is a list of goals to be considered as you expand your Master Money Plan over the months. This list is not a beginning list, but a complete overview of what a money plan can include as it develops over a period of time. It's intended as a guideline only. You are the only one who can draw up your plan.

First is a list of ideas for categories. Each category has its own separate savings account or its own separate Dream Box. Once every month, *off the top* of the paycheck, money is diversified into each goal or ¢hange is deposited regularly in Dream Boxes.

1. Financial independence account

2. Emergency account

3. Emergency future

4. Children now

5. Children future

6. Short-term goal

7. Middle-term goal

8. Long-term goal

9. Car account

10. Tax account

11. Holiday account

12. Charity/church

13. Investment account

14, 15 . . . Gardening, School, Woodworking, Music Lessons, etc.

1. Financial independence account. As this account builds over the years, so does the frequency of a good night's sleep. Since neither social security nor pension money is guaranteed, the only money you can count on is money you have put away for yourself. By saving regularly and building a formidable savings for yourself (remember the $200,000 I talked about in Chapter 2?) you give yourself a tremendous feeling of security and ultimately the freedom of financial independence. This way, if your employer goes out of business (or makes poor investments with your retirement money) or the social security well runs dry, you will still have the money you've put away for yourself. Financial independence money would include IRAs (Individual Retirement Accounts), Keoghs, tax-sheltered annuities, and any other low-risk investments you are managing that are earmarked for your own secure future.

2. Emergency account. In the beginning this is one of the first and most important accounts for many of us. It provides the immediate security many of us are lacking. This account is the first place we'll go when in a pinch. The idea is to sock away a small amount of money each month. When an emergency does arise (a new tire, medical bill, plumbing bill) this money is available and will keep us from resorting to credit cards.

3. Emergency future. This is your "sleep well" account. The goal is to accumulate a minimum of six months' take-home salary. Having this money tucked away means a good night's sleep, knowing you're prepared for a serious emergency (unemployment, prolonged illness, surgery).

4. Children now. This account prepares us for some of the larger expenses that come with raising children, such as new beds, bicycles, summer camp, braces, musical instruments. One account for all the children works well because this account is for meeting whatever needs arise rather than a gift for each child.

5. Children future. This account may be used to help with college expenses or to help your children embark on a business venture when they are mature.

6. Short-term goal. This account is critical — especially in the beginning. In order to remain inspired and motivated, we must get a taste of success early on and experience it regularly. Your short-term goal might be clothes, a small piece of furniture, weekend getaway trips, theater tickets, sporting events, jewelry, and so on.

7. Middle-term goal. This goal might take a few months or even up to a few years to achieve — for example, room remodeling, video camcorder, trip to Europe, hot tub, computer.

8. Long-term goal. Money saved in this account is for dreams and goals farther down the line. Examples of long-term goals might be a summer home, starting your own business, taking a year off from work, six months of travel.

9. Car account. Having a car account can greatly reduce our anxiety at unexpected repair bills, the cost of new tires, license tags, insurance.

10. Tax account. With this account you can relax, knowing you're prepared for that once-a-year property, business, or income tax.

11. Holiday account. For Christmas, Hanukkah, Thanksgiving, Valentine's Day. Money stashed in here throughout the year means an end to holiday charging and the start of guilt-free celebrations.

12. Charity/church. Most of my life the money I gave to charity was money I really needed for myself and my family. Since we lived on the brink, one or two major financial emergencies would have had us turning to charity for help. I finally chose to slow down on my financial giving until I had built a base for myself. With a separate account, you can make sure you have money to donate that is guilt free.

13. Investment account. A *small* amount of money each month diverted into an investment account will build slowly over the years while you're getting your financial act together. Then, when you're financially solid enough to begin taking risks, you'll have some money to gamble (invest) with.

14, 15, and so on, will be separate accounts you create to meet your needs and help you attain your goals.

These numbered categories are designed to give you an idea of how to cover all the bases. Each time we establish an account to fill a need or a goal, we're giving ourselves the incredible gifts of anticipation and control of our lives.

Here's how Kathy uses one of her goal accounts to help her feel in control. "After determining the actual cost of my vacation, I save one-twelfth of the total every month by payroll deduction. I *love* being able to start saving and planning for the next trip when I get home from this year's vacation." By planning ahead for these special once-a-year occasions, we eliminate needless anxiety and sleep well each night knowing that we're prepared.

Mary Ann said, "Everybody at work is looking at Christmas coming up, and whine, whine, whine, 'Only two paychecks until Christmas.' I don't have to worry about Christmas. It's not even a concern because I was thinking Christmas all year and I've got things put away. I watched for sales, and used cash that I had available. I'm not going to be in debt for Christmas."

What's the difference between a daydream and a goal? A daydream is an aimless thought, while goals are clearly defined and attainable. When we set a goal, we're painting ourselves a finish line that we can see. It challenges us, beckons us to make it to the end. It's the difference between thoughtlessly tossing loose ¢hange on top of the dresser or *deliberately* directing the money into our labeled Dream Box. The daydream never evolves, while a goal is a specific target that keeps us focused all the way to the finish line.

How many times have we plunked a big chunk of money into savings at the beginning of the month only to haul it back out by the end? Most of us are so eager finally to get our act together with money that we set up a lofty plan, one we can't possibly carry out. This time it's going to be different. This time our plan will be realistic and fun. No more self-sabotaging, grandiose, impossible-to-carry-out plans. As Jim said, "That's what has always derailed me in the past, setting up goals that can't possibly be reached."

Here's an example of what a first, three-month Master Money Plan might look like:

Emergency account $5 (per month)
Movie account   Dream Box (Change Game)

This plan promises to diversify money two ways: 1) $5 will come *off the top of the paycheck* each month and go directly into an emergency account, and 2) all loose change will be gathered and stashed in the Dream Box for guilt-free fun at the movies. When I speak of an emergency account, I'm talking about expenses that pop up unexpectedly and catch us unprepared. I've used my emergency account money for furnace repair, new tires, sewer clean-out, and even to buy both of my kids shoes on the same day. I try not to touch my emergency account so that it can build up; but if I need money, *that* is where I go (*not* to my Hawaii account).

The above plan is what I call realistic, motivating, and almost certain to be carried out. Each day as we slip money into our Dream Box, we *feel* the excitement, we're anticipating which movie we will see and which friend to invite to come along. Simultaneously we're building our emergency account and watching it grow — $5, $10, $15, $20. We want this fund to keep increasing, so we're trying our best not to dip into it. We're on our way.

By creating and putting a plan into action we've created momentum. What's dramatically different from what we've attempted in the past is that this plan is *doable.* We're pacing ourselves like the tortoise. We've laid out a realistic, balanced plan that we can carry out. This time there's no stopping us.

Whatever plan you design for yourself, I suggest that you keep it for three months and then reevaluate it. What will happen at the end of three months is that you'll pat yourself on the back and say something like, "This was so easy. I have fifteen dollars in my emergency fund and I've been to the movies six times!" Then you'll probably open another account at your credit union — maybe to help cover the never-ending car expenses. Before long you'll find yourself labeling another Dream Box and playing another game. Perhaps this time your goal is the trip to Australia you've always dreamed of. As the fourth month begins your new plan may look like this:

Emergency account	$12.50 (per month)
Car account	$10.00 (per month)
Movies	¢hange Game
Australia	The Extra Money Game (Chapter 5)

This revised plan will also be in operation for three months. It's a smart, realistic plan and very likely to be carried out. The biggest pitfall for most of us is making our plans too grandiose. We unrealistically list six or seven goals and try depositing $30 into each account in our desperate attempt to make up for lost time. It's too much, too soon. We can't afford that much money in six accounts, and so we fail.

Not this time. The plan you create will succeed because you're starting small and realistically. Think about it. How long have you been without a plan that works? How long have you been feeling out of control with your money? For most, the answer is "always" or "as long as I can remember." So rather than ruin this chance to finally have your dreams coming true and money saved — we're going to start slowly and surely. Imagine looking back in just three months and claiming, "I did it! My money's growing and my dreams are coming true. I am in control at last."

Any person who designs a plan similar to the one above

is practically *guaranteed* success. It's important to reevaluate your plan every three months. At that time, 1) check to see if the goals you've chosen are still your top priorities, 2) add new accounts or Dream Boxes, 3) restructure, if need be, the amount of money going into your various accounts, and 4) commit more money toward your goals, *if that's realistic.* With a money plan in action you'll experience anticipation and satisfaction every day. Your money is building, you're reaching your goals, and you're experiencing a growing feeling of satisfaction that accompanies being in control of your life.

FIVE KEYS TO CREATING A MONEY PLAN THAT TAKES YOU ALL THE WAY TO YOUR GOALS

1. Pinpointing goals that are **fun and motivating.**
2. **Starting.**
3. **Starting small.** (Remember, it's better to start right away to do the right thing than it is to wait until you think you can do it just right.)
4. **Being realistic.** ($5 saved each month and accumulated for a year is 100% better than putting away $60 today, becoming strapped for money, and withdrawing it.)
5. **Sticking to your plan no matter what.** (Keep the plan for three months and then reevaluate, adding goals, diversifying, and making changes. Continue with your revised plan for the next three months and so on.)

"For me, the biggest thing that I have noticed is that I feel better about myself, because I now have a plan for my money," writes Dave. "I have opened separate savings accounts — each with a specific purpose. Now, emergencies, or just unexpected expenses, are taken care of without 'the big squeeze.'"

A heartwarming story about starting and being realistic came from Dawn, a young mother with a two-year-old son. Newly divorced and going through bankruptcy, she writes, "My son Brandon loves to go out to a fast-food place for a kid's meal, so now, as soon as we have enough change in the jar, we go out for a treat. It's so much fun!"

When people take my workshops, I often ask them to fill out an anonymous questionnaire relating their financial situation. Can you guess what the *one* resounding common denominator is? *Lack of savings.* Most people don't have enough money to handle a large car-repair bill, an emergency flight to be with a sick relative, and the need for a new refrigerator all in the same month.

But starting a serious savings program is *not* the answer. I've tried it, you've tried it. It hasn't worked. The idea is to try something that's proven to work. If the first time you stand up to the plate with a bat in your hand, you hit a home run, at least two things happen — you like baseball and you feel successful. That's exactly what our plans must be certain to do, provide success and be fun and motivating to carry out.

To begin, jot down the one thing that is most motivating to you right now. (For me it's the trip my children and I are planning to Washington, D.C.) When we allow ourselves to focus on just one motivating idea, we've directed our energy. This concentration greatly increases our chances of success. (We're more likely to make a powerful hit when we concentrate on the ball, rather than on the fans, our form, or the coach.)

Hopefully, you've already labeled a container and been playing the ¢hange Game since you first read about it in Chapter 1. If so, you know the wonderful feelings of excitement and anticipation that go along with actually putting a plan into action. If not, I encourage you to enjoy the rewards of the ¢hange Game for a while before embarking on your Master Money Plan.

Here's what Mary, an editor and freelance writer, wrote at the end of the money workshop. "I have strengthened my purposes in life and feel more powerful about deciding each day: bagel or boots? yogurt or Europe? I know I can look ahead to fun purchases, not behind to paying off installment debt." Here is Mary's original three-month Master Money Plan:

Hiking boots	¢hange Game
Emergency account	$30 per month
Europe	10% of freelance money and all of tax return money
Computer	$10 per month

Here's what Mary's Master Money Plan looked like one year later:

Hiking boots	¢hange game. Mary explained that although she achieved the goal of buying hiking boots a long time ago, she still fondly calls it her "hiking boots fund." Right now she is saving her ¢hange for a waterproof outdoor jacket.
Emergency account	$30 per month. (This account had $651 in it the day I talked with Mary. She told me she's uncomfortable with this amount, as she likes to keep the bal-

ance at over $1,000. I asked her how much she had in her "emergency account" savings when she left class. "Zero!" She laughed. Also, she explained that she now throws all "surprise" money into this account. "Like when someone who owes me money suddenly becomes responsible and pays me back!" Remember, the emergency account is the one that it's *okay to dip into* when an unforeseen expense arises.

Europe account
The source for this account changed. Mary explained to me that each month she receives half of a mortgage payment from the home she and her former husband sold. "My partner, David, and I realized we could travel a lot sooner than we thought by directing this mortgage income to our Europe account. Before our realization, that money used to fly away like a flock of birds!"

Computer account
$10 per month: "Before I took your class I thought you only had one account and that's what you use for everything. That one account of mine had some money in there already, so that's the one we named "computer account." We bought the computer last March and now we each continue to put ten dollars a month in there which we use for computer items such as software and program updates."

Weekend fun
"We opened this account after about four months. It's our weekend getaway money. David puts in ten dollars every month, but I really vary. If we're feeling really stressed and feel like we need some fun, we'll each deposit thirty or even sixty dollars into this account."

Mary added what she called a very "qualitative" remark about the big difference in her sons' lives. "I have two sons, ages twenty-one and twenty-three. My talking with them about what I've learned has really made a difference. The other day my son asked, 'How can you go to Europe next October? You didn't used to have any money.' 'Well, remember my new life with money that I've been telling you about?'" Then, she said, he wanted to know a lot more about it.

Following is the Master Money Plan Caroline designed for herself. Notice how she's taken care to plan emergency savings for now *and* later in addition to building anticipation into her life with her three "personal fun" accounts. Her plan is well rounded and likely to be very satisfying. A motivational plan like this one is almost bound to succeed.

Three-month plan

Emergency account	$40
Emergency future	$10
Sailing/biking	$15
Europe	$30
Computer/school	$ 5

Figuring out what's best for her has been the most confusing, writes Caroline. "But now that I've actually written down my plan, my goals seem much more obtainable. I feel more at ease with myself now that I can spend the money on me and not on things I don't want. With the idea of emergency funds I feel more confident that I don't need to worry about money when I'm looking for a new job or deciding to go back to school."

Next let's review Connie's three-month money plan. It's easy to see that she has carefully based her plan on what she values. It's realistic, balanced, and motivating — and very likely to be carried out.

School	$20
Emergency account	$20
Trip to visit my sister in Israel	$10
New down comforter	¢hange Game

Notice how Connie has prioritized and weighted her goals. Even though I introduced a long list of suggested goals, including financial independence, taxes, emergency future, and a car account, Connie has carefully constructed a balanced plan based on her present needs and goals. Most important of all, because her plan recognizes what's most motivating to her just now in her life, she has greatly increased her chances of succeeding in the first three months of her plan.

I can't emphasize this enough: If you design a plan for yourself that you *love* and can easily carry out, I can practically guarantee that you will be unstoppable. Once you've tasted success, you will be a changed person. No matter what life throws your way, you'll have that solid belief that you can handle it. Vicki relayed this knowledge in her letter. "At times I felt my world was crumbling around me, but I think knowing that at least this one area of my life (finances) was stable gave me reassurance. It also made me feel good about what I had accomplished and the positive changes I had made."

When Julie relapsed she was able to catch herself. "After a while I kind of got plastic crazy again. I had grabbed the concept of paying myself first and had gone from my original goal of saving fifty dollars to saving three hundred a month. So I asked myself, 'What's wrong with this picture? If I can save three hundred a month, why am I using plastic?' It got real easy again for some reason, and clothes are so darn expensive. Within about three to four months I whomped my credit card accounts back up again. When I lost control, I looked at the whole situation and said, 'You know, this is really stupid, why are you doing this?' and I started on this recovery process."

The examples of money plans you've seen give you an idea of how to get started. Next is a money chart to give you some added incentive. This chart had quite an impact on me and gave me the perspective and inspiration I needed to stick to my plan. To make sense of the chart, let's pretend we have a newborn child and we've decided to save money for the child's future. We begin by depositing $100 each month and continue sending $100 every month to that account until our child is eighteen years old. We notice we've accumulated over $30,000 dollars in the account (exactly $31,664).

Now, instead of depositing money, we *withdraw* $100 each and every month from that account and send it to our child to help with college or in getting established. We continue withdrawing and sending $100 to our child every month for the same number of years that we have saved. After eighteen years of depleting this account by $100 a month, our balance is $33,373 — that's $1,709 *more* in the account now than when we started withdrawing!

To see how this is possible, let's take a look at the third column of the second money chart, which shows the growth

The First 18 Years—*Saving $100 Every Month*

Year	Amount Saved Yearly Depositing $100/month	Interest Added While Saving	Total in Account
1	$1,200	$ 26	$ 1,226
2	1,200	77	2,503
3	1,200	128	3,831
4	1,200	182	5,213
5	1,200	239	6,652
6	1,200	297	8,149
7	1,200	359	9,708
8	1,200	421	11,329
9	1,200	488	13,017
10	1,200	557	14,774
11	1,200	628	16,602
12	1,200	703	18,505
13	1,200	780	20,485
14	1,200	861	22,546
15	1,200	945	24,691
16	1,200	1,032	26,923
17	1,200	1,124	29,247
18	1,200	1,217	31,664

of interest. The first year after our child turned eighteen, we withdrew $1,200, while the account earned $1,266 in interest. During the eighteenth year, when we withdrew $1,200 for our child, the account earned $1,330. Because of the large sum of money earning interest, $1,330 was added to the account, even though we withdrew $1,200 and made no deposits. If you were able to average just one interest point more during these two eighteen-year periods (5% instead of 4%), your account balance would be $51,022 instead of $33,373

The Second 18 Years—*Withdrawing* $100 Every Month

Year	Amount Withdrawn Yearly Subtracting $100/month	Interest Added While Saving	Total in Account
1	$1,200	$1,266	$31,730
2	1,200	1,269	31,799
3	1,200	1,272	31,871
4	1,200	1,275	31,946
5	1,200	1,278	32,024
6	1,200	1,281	32,105
7	1,200	1,284	32,189
8	1,200	1,288	32,277
9	1,200	1,291	32,368
10	1,200	1,295	32,463
11	1,200	1,299	32,562
12	1,200	1,303	32,665
13	1,200	1,307	32,772
14	1,200	1,311	32,883
15	1,200	1,315	32,998
16	1,200	1,320	33,118
17	1,200	1,325	33,243
18	1,200	1,330	33,373

Note: This projection is based on an annual interest rate of 4%.

— that's an additional $17,649 in your pocket. Not only have you helped your child out, you've also built $51,022 worth of savings for yourself!

This chart gives us a vivid picture of why we want to (1) start now, (2) deposit money regularly, and (3) have a lump sum of money at work for us. Here's how Val put this in practice in her life. "I started saving for a trip to Europe five years before I actually went. A small amount of money out of my check every month built into a sizable sum after five years. The part that's the most fun is thinking that the interest earned on the account almost paid for my plane ticket! Also, your compound-interest charts really got me started saving toward retirement. It's exciting to see the total grow all by itself!"

One of my favorite quotes is from an author, Rusty Berkus, "Perhaps you have lived another's dream and not your own." How about you? Have you been living someone else's dream? At the time when Joy came to me for consultation, she was also coping with leaving a destructive relationship. As we talked she exclaimed, "I've spent the last thirty-three years providing *others* with goals!" Certainly that was me, too. I had never seriously looked at my dreams, much less attempted to make them come true. As a child my daily goal was to bring happiness to our tension-packed, dysfunctional family. Then, as an adult, I continued my mission and attempted for more than eighteen years to make my husband happy. I failed on all accounts. It wasn't until I turned my energy toward someone whose happiness I *did* have control over — myself — that my life began to be transformed. Opening the door to my dreams and then giving myself permission to make them happen changed the course of my entire life.

"I'm realizing the power of starting," wrote Jennie. "That it's not the amount but the experience of having an amount, any amount, set aside. Putting myself first is an issue. I noticed that everything on my plan was needs based — emergency funds, IRA, and so on, and excluded any plan for something *I* want. I was kind of scared to put in a long-term goal because I still can't afford it. Not true. I can do five dollars a month, probably easily."

As Barbara finalized her Master Money Plan, she had $5,300 in credit card debt, nothing in savings, and an annual income of $26,000. She wrote, "I'm feeling excited about eventually having the money to get what I want. I'm feeling more empowered about having choices in general in my life." Let's look at Barbara's money plan. She made a complete list of her goals. But for the first three months she put only *some* of them into action (note the six goals marked by bullets). She's being wise by starting small, taking only $30 off the top of her paycheck each month. Over time she can slowly and realistically incorporate the rest of her plan. For added incentive she's put one-third of her money toward the fun goal of a Colorado trip that will help keep her motivated and on track.

Retirement (IRA)	
✦ Emergency account	$ 5
✦ Emergency future	$ 5
✦ School tuition	$10
✦ Colorado trip	$10
New Mexico trip	
Trip to Europe	
Investment	
✦ Boom box	¢hange Game
✦ Christmas presents	¢hange Game

USING YOUR MASTER MONEY PLAN SHEET

I heartily encourage you to go to a copy machine and enlarge the Master Money Plan sheet located on pages 188–189. This sheet is a powerful tool. I hope you choose to put it to use.

Before you begin filling out your plan, take time to list what you value most in life. Keep your sheet of paper handy throughout the day. As the dreams and goals you have longed for over the years pop into your head, jot them down. When your brainstorming list of "what matters most to you in life" feels complete, look it over and mark the ones that have particular meaning and significance at this point in your life. Once you've zeroed in on what moves you the most, you're ready to proceed.

1. Begin filling out your Master Money Plan sheet by listing your goals beneath the bold words "My Goals" found near the upper left of the page.

2. On the far left of the upper section, in the column headed "My Monthly $ Commitment to My Goals," begin penciling in the *realistic* amount of money you promise to put toward each goal each month. Place a dollar amount beside only the goals you are actually going to put into action during these next three months. Remember, some of your goals will be funded by the money games you'll be playing (and winning!) instead of a dollar amount from the paycheck.

3. The third column, labeled "Account # or Name of Game" is the place to record the account number given to you by your credit union or bank. Now when your statement arrives you can match the number on the statement with your goal and update your records as interest is added to your accounts.

4. Let's pretend it's March. After you've actually deposited the amount you promised yourself (let's say $15), enter

the $15 off to the right of the goal under the column headed "March." A month goes by and now it's April. After you've deposited $15 for April, add the new $15 to the previous total ($15) and enter the total amount of money in that account (in this case $30) in the column for April.

Remember, it's very important that we write dollar amounts on our plan sheet only after we have safely tucked the money away for our goal. That way, when we enter the new total for our goal, it is real — we've actually set the money aside and we can bask in the feeling of pride and success as we write.

Every new deposit for our goals means a new or updated entry on our Master Money Plan sheet and the emotional charge of watching our money grow: $15, $30, $45, $60. For the first time in our lives (for many of us), as we glance across our Master Money Plan sheet, we can actually *see* our money growing.

5. Another great boost and positive feeling comes when we see and experience what is happening at the bottom of the Master Money Plan sheet. First, at the bottom on the far left under "Installment Bills," list your credit card, car loan, and any other installment bills. Then, just to the right of the list of bills enter the total balance of each bill. Each month as you pay the minimum amount due, subtract your payment from the total. As you look across the bottom of the page, you'll feel encouraged and relieved as you watch your credit card balances going down, down, down. One of the reasons I always use a pencil is that when I pay the minimum, I like to subtract the amount I paid, for example, a $702.42 balance minus my

minimum payment of $21 equals a new credit card balance of $681.42. Of course when the next bill arrives it has interest charges added, so I merely erase the previous figure and make the adjustment.

6. We can also use the Master Money Plan sheet to find out how much money we have saved altogether by looking at the current month and adding down that column. We're adding together the total of each goal and giving ourselves a grand total, or net worth. I get a charge out of doing that from time to time because, as I look at my accounts individually, the totals might be $27.19 and $54.98 and $105.73 and $44.37. And that feels good. But to realize that all together I've saved $232.27 can really spur me on!

7. By actually sitting down with our Master Money Plan sheet at our once-a-month bill-paying time each month, we give ourselves the lift of seeing our entire money plan falling into place. You'll find yourself looking forward to this day because you are (1) paying yourself first, diversifying that money into your goals, and seeing the totals growing, (2) paying the minimum on your installment bills and watching them go away, and (3) rejoicing in the newfound freedom of taking charge of your money and your life.

8. Seeing progress is what keeps us going; thus the Master Money Plan sheet can be a tremendous aid in helping us achieve our goals. Use it. Keep it handy. Give yourself the satisfaction of seeing your progress. Keep a pencil nearby so you

MASTER MONEY PLAN

My Monthly $ Commitment to My Goals	What I *Really* Want in Life **MY GOALS**	Account # or Name of Game	Jan. +	Feb. +	Mar. +	Apr. +

Installment Bills	Enter Total Amount Due.				

> When I *don't* use
> my credit cards
> and when I *pay*
> *the minimum* $
> due, I have money
> for my goals and I
> can see the bills
> disappearing!

MASTER MONEY PLAN *(continued)*

May +	June +	July +	Aug. +	Sept. +	Oct. +	Nov. +	Dec. +

(Each month as you pay the *minimum* amount due, *subtract* your payment from the total
and watch the balance due *disappear.*)

Values ➺ **Choices** ➺ ACTION

I tune in to what I **value** most in life.
I make my **choices** carefully, *based* on what I value.
I **act** according to the values that bring me deep inner satisfaction.

---

can erase and "up" the totals as you funnel more money into an account.

Bonnie, married with three children, said, "I took money out of every check for our family trip to Minnesota. I knew that the little bit of money I set aside wouldn't be enough by itself but that over time it would build. I could plan out each step and exactly how long it would take before I could take the trip. Putting money in frequently is what keeps me interested and keeps me doing it.

"It makes me feel like I don't have to wait to have fun, I've got it now. I have all that fun anticipating. And it makes the vacation or whatever it is more enjoyable, too. I find that if I've anticipated something and then get to do it, it's much more pleasurable than if it just happens."

I received a call from Daniel about my lectures. After re-marking on the fact that his last name is Italian, I asked if he was saving his ¢hange for a trip to Italy. Daniel answered, "As a divorced dad with two little girls I have no money for vacations and adventures like that." How does that statement sound to you now? Has there been a shift in you?

WRITING YOUR PLAN

It's time to write down your plan — values ➤ choice ➤ action. It's tricky designing a foolproof, guaranteed-to-succeed plan. Here are some guidelines to help ensure your success.

1. Be Realistic: Whatever amount of money you've been considering setting aside each month for your plan — cut the amount *in half.* For example:

Shaky Plan		Revised (cut-in-half) SOLID Plan	
Emergency account	$40	Emergency account	$20
Car account	$10	Car account	$ 5
Ocean weekend	$20	Ocean weekend	$10
New clothes	¢hange Game	New clothes	¢hange Game

It's tough to cut our planned amounts of money in half because we're excited to finally get going. But I encourage you to do it. Remember, you can always do as Tom did ($13,000 in savings in a year and a half). He left class with a plan to deposit $5 into each of his four accounts every month ($20 total). What actually happened was that as the months went by he sent an extra $30 off to this account and an extra $50 off to that account. This approach is the way to go because you've built in a safety net. If after two months Tom had suddenly needed $200, he could have withdrawn each of his accounts back to $10 with no guilt because his promise to himself was $5 a month.

Relax. Start slowly. But start — that's the key. Remind yourself how long you have been operating with no plan at all. Then, take a deep breath and put into operation a simple, realistic plan. Three months will fly by before you know it.

Kelly attended just one section of a three-part money workshop. When I saw him later, he hesitantly explained that he had taken $200 off the top of his next paycheck and put it in savings. So why was he feeling awkward? In a family of five, with substantial credit card debt, he couldn't possibly afford to take $200 out of the family funds and within two weeks the money was back out again. If he had come to the rest of the seminar, he would have learned how important it is to start small and be realistic!

2. Build your plan around fun. It's essential that your plan is enticing and exciting. It must be so much fun that you stick to it no matter what. Later, after you're "hooked" and are in the habit of paying yourself first, then you can add the more "responsible" accounts.

3. Keep your plan for three months.

4. Remember, doing something is better than doing nothing — a whole lot better. If two days from now you still haven't written down your plan — you probably never will. Sketch out your plan right now, finalize it within two days, and put it into action first thing next payday. *Pay yourself first* — before you pay money for anything else. It's *your* money.

5. Your plan must feel good. After you have listed all your goals and chosen the one or two that you will be contributing to for the next three months, sit back and give each chosen goal "emotional weight." In other words ask yourself, "If I were going to start with only one goal, which would make me feel the best?" When people are in their fifties or sixties, what often feels best is to start their own Individual Retirement Account (IRA). Knowing they'll have some security gives them tremendous peace and satisfaction. For people raising children, the emergency account is likely to get the most weight, and a young, single career person might put a travel account in first place. Do what is most rewarding and motivating for you right now in your life.

6. Balance your plan. Your plan must include security money *and* fun money in order to work. Security money helps us sleep peacefully, while fun money gives us a reason to bound out of bed in the morning. Check and double-check that you have weighted your plan based on the fun and security that will motivate you most today. We're not making a "responsible" plan or a plan to impress anyone. The key to finally breaking out of our old ways with money is to succeed in reaching our goals. Many people (myself included) began their three-month plan with only one goal in operation and played the ¢hange Game to achieve it.

MONEY CHARTS

Unlike money charts that are intimidating or mind-boggling, I've inserted the money charts that follow to make planning your goals more fun and to give you incentive.

Let's say you figure out that you need about $500 to reach your goal. Flip to the money charts and begin looking across and down the columns for "$500." Start at the top left of the first chart and move across until you find $20 a month. Then, move down the column and you'll find $501. That figure means that if you deposit $20 every month (earning 4% interest), at the end of two years you'll have $501. Now move farther to the right in the top column to a $50 a month deposit. You see that in just one year you'll have saved $613.

HOW MONTHLY SAVINGS GROW

Pay Attention to Interest Rates!

	$5.00 4.00%	$5.00 8.00%	$10.00 4.00%	$10.00 8.00%	$20.00 4.00%	$35.00 4.00%	$50.00 4.00%
1	$61	$63	$123	$125	$245	$429	$613
2	125	131	250	261	501	876	1,251
3	192	204	383	408	766	1,341	1,915
4	261	284	521	567	1,043	1,825	2,607
5	333	370	665	740	1,330	2,328	3,326
6	407	463	815	926	1,630	2,852	4,075
7	485	564	971	1,129	1,942	3,398	4,854
8	566	674	1,133	1,348	2,266	3,965	5,665
9	651	792	1,302	1,585	2,603	4,556	6,509
10	739	921	1,477	1,842	2,955	5,171	7,387
11	830	1,060	1,660	2,120	3,320	5,811	8,301
12	925	1,211	1,851	2,421	3,701	6,477	9,253
13	1,024	1,374	2,049	2,747	4,097	7,170	10,243
14	1,127	1,550	2,255	3,101	4,509	7,891	11,273
15	1,235	1,742	2,469	3,483	4,938	8,642	12,346
16	1,346	1,949	2,692	3,898	5,385	9,423	13,462

17	1,462	2,173	2,925	4,347	5,849	10,236	14,623
18	1,583	2,416	3,166	4,833	6,333	11,083	15,832
19	1,709	2,680	3,418	5,359	6,836	11,963	17,090
20	1,840	2,965	3,680	5,929	7,360	12,880	18,400
21	1,976	3,273	3,953	6,547	7,905	13,834	19,763
22	2,118	3,608	4,235	7,216	8,472	14,827	21,181
23	2,266	3,970	4,531	7,940	9,063	15,860	22,657
24	2,419	4,362	4,839	8,724	9,677	16,935	24,193
25	2,579	4,787	5,158	9,574	10,317	18,055	25,792
26	2,746	5,247	5,491	10,494	10,982	19,219	27,456
27	2,919	5,745	5,838	11,490	11,675	20,432	29,188
28	3,099	6,284	6,198	12,569	12,396	21,693	30,990
29	3,287	6,869	6,573	13,737	13,146	23,006	32,866
30	3,482	7,501	6,964	15,003	13,927	24,373	34,818
31	3,685	8,187	7,370	16,374	14,740	25,795	36,850
32	3,896	8,929	7,793	17,858	15,586	27,275	38,964
33	4,116	9,733	8,233	19,465	16,466	28,815	41,165
34	4,346	10,603	8,691	21,206	17,382	30,419	43,455
35	4,584	11,546	9,168	23,092	18,336	32,087	45,839
36	4,832	12,567	9,664	25,134	19,328	33,824	48,320
37	5,090	13,673	10,180	27,345	20,361	35,631	50,901
38	5,359	14,870	10,718	29,740	21,435	37,512	53,588
39	5,638	16,167	11,277	32,334	22,554	39,469	56,385
40	5,930	17,571	11,859	35,143	23,718	41,507	59,295

HOW MONTHLY SAVINGS GROW

Pay Attention to Interest Rates!

	$50.00 8.00%	$50.00 12.00%	$100.00 3.00%	$100.00 5.50%	$100.00 10.00%	$250.00 4.00%	$250.00 8.00%
1	$627	$640	$1,220	$1,236	$1,267	$3,066	$3,133
2	1,305	1,362	2,476	2,542	2,667	6,257	6,527
3	2,040	2,175	3,771	3,922	4,213	9,577	10,201
4	2,836	3,092	5,106	5,380	5,921	13,033	14,181
5	3,698	4,124	6,481	6,920	7,808	16,630	18,492
6	4,632	5,288	7,898	8,546	9,893	20,373	23,160
7	5,643	6,599	9,358	10,265	12,196	24,269	28,215
8	6,738	8,076	10,862	12,080	14,740	28,324	33,690
9	7,924	9,741	12,412	13,998	17,550	32,543	39,620
10	9,208	11,617	14,009	16,024	20,655	36,935	46,041
11	10,599	13,731	15,655	18,164	24,085	41,506	52,996
12	12,106	16,113	17,351	20,425	27,874	46,263	60,528
13	13,737	18,797	19,098	22,814	32,060	51,213	68,685
14	15,504	21,821	20,899	25,337	36,684	56,365	77,519
15	17,417	25,229	22,754	28,002	41,792	61,728	87,086
16	19,490	29,069	24,666	30,818	47,436	67,308	97,448

17	21,734	33,396	26,636	33,793	53,670	73,116	108,669
18	24,164	38,272	28,666	36,936	60,557	79,161	120,822
19	26,797	43,766	30,757	40,255	68,165	85,452	133,983
20	29,647	49,957	32,912	43,762	76,570	91,999	148,237
21	32,735	56,934	35,133	47,467	85,855	98,813	163,674
22	36,078	64,795	37,421	51,381	96,112	105,905	180,392
23	39,699	73,653	39,779	55,516	107,443	113,285	198,497
24	43,621	83,634	42,209	59,884	119,961	120,967	218,106
25	47,868	94,882	44,712	64,498	133,789	128,961	239,342
26	52,468	107,556	47,292	69,373	149,066	137,281	262,340
27	57,449	121,837	49,950	74,522	165,942	145,940	287,247
28	62,844	137,929	52,689	79,962	184,585	154,951	314,222
29	68,687	156,063	55,511	85,709	205,180	164,330	343,436
30	75,015	176,496	58,419	91,780	227,933	174,091	375,074
31	81,868	199,520	61,416	98,193	253,067	184,249	409,338
32	89,289	225,465	64,504	104,969	280,834	194,822	446,446
33	97,327	254,700	67,685	112,126	311,508	205,825	486,634
34	106,032	287,643	70,964	119,687	345,393	217,276	530,158
35	115,459	324,763	74,342	127,675	382,828	229,194	577,294
36	125,668	366,592	77,823	136,113	424,182	241,598	628,342
37	136,725	413,726	81,409	145,027	469,866	254,507	683,627
38	148,700	466,837	85,105	154,444	520,334	267,941	743,501
39	161,669	526,684	88,913	164,393	576,087	281,924	808,345
40	175,714	594,121	92,837	174,902	637,678	296,475	878,570

But maybe you're not in a hurry, perhaps this is a long-term goal you are planning. You notice that by saving just $10 a month at 4% you'll have $521 in four years (or $567 at 8% interest).

Earmark these pages of money charts and have fun with them. Move your eyes across and down the page, remaining open to various angles and approaches until you come up with a plan for saving for your goals that feels best to you. Let the charts help motivate you to reach for the stars.

These charts are excellent for reminding us why we want to start *today* to save. At the top of the second chart find $100 a month. If we began at age twenty-five to save $100 a month at 3%, we'd have $92,837 saved when we turned sixty-five. At 5.5% average interest earned over the forty years, we'd have $174,902. If, however, during those forty years of socking away $100 every month, we paid close attention to getting the highest (safe) interest possible and averaged 10% over the years, we'd have $637,678.

Big numbers boggle my mind, so let me put this another way. Let's say that after forty years of saving money, you retire and plan to begin living off the money you've saved. First of all it's very important not to withdraw any of the lump sum of money you've accumulated. The whole idea is to leave that large amount alone and live off the interest it generates. Think about it. If you were accustomed to living on $40,000 a year and depleted that amount from your total savings each year, your money would be gone in just a few years and then what would you do?

Let's look and see how much interest income we might expect to keep receiving year after year from the money we've saved.

Total Saved over a 40-Year Period	Interest Rate	Annual Interest Income	Monthly Interest Income
$ 92,837	3%	$ 2,785	$ 232
174,902	3%	5,247	437
637,678	3%	19,130	1,594
92,837	5%	4,641	386
174,902	5%	8,745	728
637,678	5%	31,883	2,657
92,837	8%	7,426	618
174,902	8%	13,992	1,166
637,678	8%	51,014	4,251

Remember that the numbers in the left-hand column titled "Total Saved" came from saving $100 a month for forty years. The higher the interest earned over the years, the higher the total.

The dramatic differences in the monthly income amaze me. It drives the point home — pay attention to interest rates. Take a few minutes a couple of times a year to make certain your hard-to-come-by money is placed in the credit union, bank, or low-risk investment offering the highest interest.

TIPS

Following are a variety of tips and ideas to assist you in creating and sticking to your plan.

✦ **Payroll deduction and direct deposit.** If your employer offers the option of payroll deduction and direct deposit,

you to consider taking advantage of it. It is a tre-
rvice to you and a great way to help you with your
money management. Payroll deduction and direct deposit are
electronic transfer procedures in which your paycheck is deposited directly into your account at your credit union or bank
on payday. You no longer have to carry your paycheck around
with you trying to make time to drive to the bank, and your
money begins earning interest the moment you're paid. Your
credit union (or bank) will automatically diversify your money
into your various goal accounts — all you need to do is fill out
a form to let them know how much money to direct into
which account. When I want to add or change the amounts
going into my various goal accounts, I just give the credit
union a call. With automatic diversification taking place at
the bank, all I do at home is enter the additional amounts
on my Master Money Plan sheet — the money is already in
the account.

✦ **What's a C.D.?** A certificate of deposit (C.D.) is a specific kind of savings account that usually provides higher interest than regular savings because you agree to leave the
money in the bank for a period of time (for example, three
months, six months, one year, three years, and so on). Certifi-
cates of deposit are a good place for our long-term goals and
emergency future money. Although the money in the C.D. is
yours and you can withdraw it at any time, you will be
charged a small penalty if you withdraw before the agreed-
upon maturity date of the C.D.

✦ **Write a personal money statement.** Help yourself
lock into your plan and this new approach to money by writ-

ing a personal money statement at the top of your Master Money Plan sheet. Here's what Dave, age twenty-five, wrote. "I am learning to make my money work for *me*. I am on my way to financial independence. My goal for the future: to be able to go where I want, when I want, with my family and *not* have to worry about money!" Be sure to write in a positive, upbeat, *present-tense* voice. Notice that Dave wrote, "I am," not "I will." Emotionally it's important for us to use words that tell our psyche that it *is* happening, not that it's going to happen at some unknown date in the future. In other words, say, "I *am* paying myself first" instead of, "I'm *going* to pay myself first." Refer to the affirmations on page 228 for ideas.

✦ **Do what works.** Joanne told me, "I just gave my sister five hundred dollars to keep for me." That's the idea. Be creative and enlist all the help you can get. Do whatever works to make certain you reach your goals.

✦ **Plan ahead.** Figure out ahead of time how you will divide up unexpected (or expected) money. For example, you might decide to divide up smaller amounts of money like this: 60% of the amount for your most passionate goal and 40% for your emergency account. Larger amounts of money might be diversified even further, for example, 20% for the emergency account, 60% divided among short-term, middle-term, and long-term goals, and 20% to go into the general fund to help get through the month.

When we've decided how to distribute money before we have it in hand, it makes it easier for us to be objective and good to ourselves when it arrives. I've found it very helpful to jot down my percentage plan for diversifying money right on my Master Money Plan sheet so I can easily refer to it — and then it serves as a reminder, too.

✦ **Withdraw only what you need.** It took me a long time to catch on to this next tip. When I used to transfer money from my emergency account to cover a $105.88 sewer clean-out bill, I'd say, "Please transfer $110.00 to my checking account." By rounding up the total I was depleting my emergency fund of more than the cost of the emergency. No more. If I have an emergency that costs $105.88, then that is exactly the amount of money I transfer.

✦ **Give yourself something to aim for.** Over the years I've heard financial advisors tell us to save 10% of what we make. Most of my life I dismissed the idea as impossible. Finally one day I turned the idea around and made it an *incentive* for myself. I multiplied 10% times the take-home pay (net pay), and that dollar amount became my goal. I wanted to keep upping the amount coming off the top of the paycheck until I was saving 10% of the monthly income. Once I reached that amount, my next goal became to diversify 10% of the *gross* pay (the paycheck amount before deductions). When I arrived at saving 10% of the gross, I didn't need incentives anymore — I was flying on my own.

Another incentive is to increase the amount going to our goals at a logical time each year. I clearly remember the first "raise" I gave our goals; it was in September. Since my husband was a teacher, the start of school seemed a perfect time of year to give us more money for our goals (even though we hadn't actually had a raise in years).

✦ **Family goal night.** This idea came from a couple in class who have had success with this in their family. A family goal night is an opportunity for the whole family to brainstorm ideas for individual and family goals and to set up a plan. Before trying this idea, I encourage you to have experience operating your own plan for at least three to six months. That way, when you begin suggesting ways to make family goals happen, you'll have some personal experience to go by, not just something you read about in a book. Make family goal night fun for the whole family by establishing a ground rule that any and all ideas will be accepted openly, free of criticism. Probably the first meeting or two will be for brainstorming only — getting the family thinking and open to the world of possibilities for family (and individual) goals. Keep each meeting short and fun so you'll be able to gather the family again to move a step further.

✦ **Redirect the money.** Each time you make a new choice, remember to reassign the money you *would* have spent and direct it toward your goals.

✦ **Stay with the ship.** Put your money in your goal accounts and *leave it there.* You never had it before, so act as if you don't have it now. I'm talking about what to do if two weeks or four months from now you have a big, unexpected expense. (And you probably will.) If you don't think about it ahead of time, you might be tempted to take the money you've saved for your goal and use it for the unexpected expense.

The first time this happened to me, I thought, "I've never put money away for a goal before. In fact, I've never put money away for anything before." So rather than snuff out my dreams that were just beginning to come to life, I decided to handle the emergency the same way I always had in the past, by charging, borrowing money, juggling money, having a garage sale. In other words, I handled the emergency as if I didn't have that goal money. (I have a hunch that is when I started my first emergency account.)

✦ **Make it fun.** Keep challenging yourself to make this as much fun as possible. James was so excited that he stood up in a workshop to tell us what he had done. "When I took my check to the bank, I asked for ten one-dollar bills. I brought them home and stuffed them one at a time (he demonstrated with his hands) into my mayonnaise jar labeled Motorcycle. It was great!"

✦ **Celebrate your progress all along the way.** Before dieting, we hop on a scale so we can measure our progress. On the back of your Master Money Plan sheet take just a few minutes to "weigh in" and figure out your assets and debts. Although this can be a bit scary, most of the time it ends up being surprisingly affirming. When I first decided to figure out my assets and debts, I was convinced the scale would be tilted totally toward debt, with nothing on the asset side. Happily, it wasn't as bleak as I imagined, and I've noticed that's the case for most people. We all have some assets and usually much more than we realize. (Of course our greatest asset is our wonderful self.)

Guesstimating the total in these two columns of assets and debts can take five minutes or five hours. When a suggestion like this is made, most of us begin operating from the "all or nothing" mode and opt for nothing. Instead, set the timer for five minutes, flip your Master Money Plan sheet over, and go for it. Or, fill in the blanks below. For the rest of your life you'll be able to return to these figures to measure how far you've come. You'll thank yourself over and over again for taking the few minutes to "weigh in" so that now you can celebrate the progress.

Assets		Debts	
You DO have assets!		*Just think—this column*	
		is <u>disappearing</u>!	
Item	Guesstimated Value	Item	Guesstimated Value
Today's Date:			
Car	_____	Car loan(s)	_____
Furniture	_____	Student loan(s)	_____
Tools	_____	Major credit card(s)	_____
Appliances	_____	_____ credit card	_____
Electronic		_____ credit card	_____
equipment	_____	_____ credit card	_____
Jewelry	_____	_____ credit card	_____
Clothing	_____	Bank loan(s)	_____
Sports equipment	_____	Personal loan(s)	_____
China/glassware	_____	Other loan(s)	_____
Savings	_____		_____
Cash surrender value			
life insurance	_____		_____
Stocks and bonds	_____		_____
TOTAL:	_____	**TOTAL:**	_____
Real estate		Mortgage(s) on real estate	
TOTAL:	_____	**TOTAL:**	_____

I separated real estate from the section above because real estate debt is usually long-term. The installment debt is relatively short-term. As you pay yourself first, pay the minimum on your installment bills, and stop using credit and credit cards, the previous debt column will rapidly empty.

Remember, if you take just five minutes right now to guesstimate your assets and debts, for the rest of your life you'll be able to look back at your financial situation today and celebrate how far you have come.

TIPS FOR COUPLES

1. To each his own. Each person in a relationship (or in a family) needs to have his or her own separate goal as well as joint or family goals. A sure way to create resentment and heartache in a relationship is to make one person's goal the focus of attention while shoving the other person's dream to the side. It does not work. (At least not for long.) If $10 is all you can squeeze out, then $5 goes into each person's account. As each individual experiences the satisfaction of dreams coming true, the joy experienced will be brought to the relationship. It's a win-win situation for sure.

2. Plan together. Once you've each established your own separate goals, think about planning something fun for the two of you. Sandra and Dave saved their change and spent a romantic weekend in a fancy hotel.

3. Two incomes? It's so tempting in today's society to rely on two incomes just to "get by." All too often in our quest for nicer cars and bigger homes we don't realize we've given away our freedom. Here are some reasons to stay out of the two-income trap (or work to get out of it if you're already in it): Children — if you are relying on two incomes just to make ends meet, neither parent is free to be home with the children (to raise them or to care for them during an illness). Death — if one person dies suddenly, the other is not able to maintain finances alone. Divorce — not only can the stress from the need for two paychecks add to marital conflict, it often keeps individuals in a destructive relationship because they feel financially trapped. Lack of options — one of the beautiful aspects of being in a relationship is helping support the other in meeting individual needs or goals. If a couple requires two incomes just to meet monthly expenses, tremendous stress is added to the relationship. Emotional and physical needs such as the freedom to take a break, go back to school, or change careers can't be met without major lifestyle changes.

I encourage you to try to meet your living expenses with one paycheck. Then, not only do you have freedom and increased options, but the second income can be used entirely for diversifying among all your goals.

4. Do it for you. You may be reading this book hoping that your partner will join you in trying these ideas. Unfortunately, he or she may choose not to come along for the ride. (I know, because I was alone in applying these money principles all the years I was married.) Charlene recently gave her employees a holiday bonus check. She told me one employee exclaimed, "This bonus money is for me. My partner controls all the money in the household, but this money is mine." Nancy wrote this in her final class evaluation: "I know I will save with or without my husband."

SUMMARY

Years ago, when I was creating our family's Master Money Plan, I opened an account and labeled it "emergency future." I had $30 automatically transferred to that account each month when my husband's payroll check arrived at the credit union by direct deposit. A little more than two years later the school district where my husband worked went on strike, and we were without a paycheck. The future had become the present.

Our "emergency future" money had been growing in our credit union and in a six-month certificate of deposit and had become $917. Whew. I was just able to make our $450 house payment and minimum payments to dentists and credit card companies. With simple meals of soups and pasta we made it through the month. It was a phenomenal experience for me. An *entire month* without a paycheck and we didn't use our credit cards, borrow from relatives, or dip into any of our goal accounts. The little $30 deposited faithfully every month into our emergency future account paid off big dividends. I was sold. The following month, when we had a paycheck, I upped the amount going into our emergency future account from $30 to $50 a month.

Remember, it's more important to start right away to do the right thing than it is to wait until you think you can do it just right. Drop your change in a labeled jar, stuff one-dollar bills in a labeled sock, stop at your credit union and open a specific goal account, or mail a check every month to a friend a thousand miles away. Not all. Not nothing. *Just do something.*

Go to sleep tonight with the deeply satisfying feeling of knowing you have taken action with your money — that you have made that first, essential step that will alter your entire future.

SEVEN

Summing It Up — Where Do I Go from Here?

If you have two pennies you should buy a loaf
of bread with one, which will sustain your
life, and a flower with the other, which will
give you a reason to live.
— Adapted from Mohammed

WALKING through the furniture section of a department store one day, K.W.'s daughter said, "Mom, I really want a canopy bed like that one."

"We can't afford it," responded her mom, who had taken my money workshop.

"Yes, we can!" exclaimed the seven-year-old. "All we have to do is label a jar Canopy Bed and start putting money in it. Pretty soon we'll have enough for my canopy bed!"

That's it. This seven-year-old has it figured out. She's in touch with what's important to her, and she knows what to do to make it happen. But what if a few days from now the little girl wants a pair of roller skates? Most adults would panic, saying, "Oh no, now what?" But a seven-year-old would likely take the new goal in stride. She either grabs another jar and labels it Roller Skates, or she tapes the new label Roller Skates over the old Canopy Bed. It's as simple as that.

Keeping it simple is one of the best ways to ensure your success with money and almost anything else. Here's how applying the same principle in another area of her life worked for Chris. She simply changed "I should" to "I want," and here's what happened for her. "I've lost the twelve pounds I've been struggling to shed for the past ten years. What I did was open the refrigerator with a new attitude. Instead of saying 'I *should* have carrots or celery,' I said, 'I want to fit into my clothes. I want to look good and feel good. I want to eat those things that will help me reach my goal.'" And she did.

Though what we want to do with our money is quite simple, the obstacles in our way are often monumental. It means abandoning our old familiar attitudes and patterns and stepping into the unknown of new choices. You've read that some people left the money workshop scared and reluctant, wondering, "Can I really affect my situation? Can putting nickels and dimes in a jar really amount to anything? Can something that grips and immobilizes me really be tackled in such a simple way? Let's listen to some stories to see what has happened.

As you read, pay particular attention to the energy shift people have experienced. Notice that their negative feelings about money and bills have been replaced by a positive, hope-filled spirit. Soon (if not already) you, too, will be experiencing these powerful and uplifting feelings on a regular basis.

"I found myself overwhelmed with anger," wrote Margaret, a forty-six-year-old self-employed single parent, "and rather than write something wrathful, I left your class early. When I took your class, I lived from month to month on my income, using credit cards for extraneous expenses. During the last class, you asked us to write down our feelings about what we learned. I had a burning desire to get my life in order and knew you had given me the information I needed, but I was afraid of changing. I steamed for days as I went ahead and did the prescribed program.

"I saved change, joined a credit union, and opened several accounts. Credit cards had been my 'fun.' I bought clothes with them, vacationed in Hawaii, and traveled to resorts. To live on the money I already made seemed rigidly joyless and punishing, but I was willing to try in the hopes of blossoming more at a later time.

"Eleven months have passed since that class. For the first time in my life, my quarterly taxes are paid, I have money in my checking account, I have met my children's monetary needs, credit card balances are dwindling, and I have $5,000 in savings.

"I still have a long way to go, but I can comfortably visualize it happening. What was a personal victimization was reversed into a feeling of *empowerment.* I know I will own my own home in the not too distant future. Money is being put away for my children and for me. I am going to Europe for the first time. What was only wishful thinking is now a reality. Your class helped me turn the corner into a brighter future."

Here's what Julie shared with me. "I think what grabbed me in the class the first time around was the jar of money. Saving all of your coinage for a week, and that first buzz of counting that money and saying, 'My God, I saved seven or eight or nine dollars and it hasn't been painful!' I think that you really have to be able to *hold it, smell it, and feel it;* it has to be tangible, because for many of us money has been so elusive."

Julie went on to talk about the power she has now. "If I had lost my job prior to taking your class, I probably would have had to go to my parents for money, groveling and getting hysterical. What the money I have saved has afforded me to do is sit here and wait for the right job to open up. I've got options and I've turned down several jobs. That's real powerful stuff, to say, 'I don't like your benefit package, I'm not going to work for you.' I'm not desperate. But if it had happened before, I would have taken the first thing that came along whether I liked it or not; I would have just enslaved myself."

As you read the following story, notice that Mikell seems to be feeling "free" of many negative feelings. "Now there's no guilt and no shame. There's not the terrible anxiety of always being in debt and never having enough money. There's not the awful feeling of spending too much and regretting it. I no longer have 'buyer's remorse' because now I plan what I am going to buy. I just spent a hundred and fifty dollars on something. I don't know if I need these particularly, but I do absolutely love them and they're a wonderful luxury. I was able to do that, pay my bills, save money, eat, and do all the things that I need to do. I bought myself some happiness."

As we take action, our life expands beyond anything we could have imagined. Our new choices unleash opportunities. Here's what happened for Mary Ann. "I got the brainstorm to call about a home medical transcription course. It cost four hundred and fifty dollars and *I had the cash to do it!* Before, when I was living paycheck to paycheck, I couldn't consider doing something else even though I could see my field was drying up. Now I had the option because I had the money to say, 'I can take some of this money and invest in myself.' That was a good feeling, to actually have the cash to do it. That wouldn't have been even an option a year ago.

"What's neat is I'm in control of my destiny, not the company I work for. *I* have control. Even if I lost my job tomorrow, I would still have an option. Before, I wandered around saying, 'Oh, I can't afford this, I can't afford that.' That was a lament I always had. But now I can afford it because I have money. Before I just wasn't using money right."

Other people notice the change, too. Mary Ann went on to say, "Somebody at work had gotten into some trouble with management and they told her, 'You really should do some of that stuff Mary Ann is doing because it's made a tremendous difference in her life.' Well, there's only two things that I've done, that's ACA [the twelve-step growth process for **A**dult **C**hildren of **A**lcoholics] and your seminar and they both deal with the same issue — taking charge of your life and not being a victim. Basically that's the bottom line. You don't have to be a victim to your money. As long as I'm making strides, then that's all I can ask for. My income hasn't changed all that much, but I have a lot more money.

"I'm inspired. Every day I say to myself, 'I'm in charge.' When something comes up, it's a hurdle, but it's not a downfall. I just jump over it and keep on going. Before, when I didn't have any money and had no control, a crisis was a major downfall, and I'd lose my step. Now, it's just a hurdle, and I keep right on going."

One of the biggest bonuses of this money approach is that you'll begin feeling better and seeing results quickly. Janell wrote to me just four months after attending the workshop: "I've set up a vacation account at a separate credit union that is difficult to get to, and I don't have an exchange card for that account. My plan is to take, for the first time in my life [fifty-three years], a vacation in December to Mexico that is fully paid for before I go.

"I've been saving all my change in a piggy bank which I count and deposit every two weeks. So far I've saved $78 in change. It goes to my vacation account, which already has $700 in it."

Perhaps you remember the story about Marcus from Chapter 1. During his appointment he had an "aha" experience, realizing he had been putting his bills in first place instead of his goals. Here's what Marcus had to say a year and a half later. "Without wanting to sound too melodramatic, I have to say that my life has pretty much done a one-hundred-and-eighty-degree turn.

"When I met you, Carol, fifteen or sixteen months ago, I was close to ten thousand dollars in debt with various loans and credit cards. There were times that it was really tough, and I had to do some creative financing to make sure that bills got paid on time. But the real important thing, at the root of all this, was that I wasn't happy.

"This past September I had just turned thirty, and I was going to make it real special by going to Sweden. I had the money, thanks to the Dream Box you gave me and your plan of putting aside pocket change and a few dollars here and there — it's amazing how much that amounted to. But because I don't have seniority at work, I didn't get the time off. I was disappointed, but that money is sitting, waiting for a trip to Europe this spring.

"My problem before was that I was constantly worried about paying bills. Now, as I continue to make the minimum payment, the bills are getting paid off. And I haven't incurred any new debts.

"It's taken me a long time, but something I've come to accept is the realization that as long as I'm making a change in my behavior, it doesn't matter if it doesn't show, because it will in time. A friend of mine used the example of being a hundred and twenty-five pounds overweight. He said he got really discouraged after losing his first five pounds because it didn't show. Then a friend told him, 'You know, it's kind of like a pail of sand. If you take a cup of sand out, it shows, but if you take a cup of sand off a beach, it doesn't show. But it's a cup of sand in either case, and they're just as important.' I sort of modified that for my own situation with reducing my debt. I figure five dollars today may not show, but it matters, and it will show in time."

Marcus continued, "What has happened for me is really profound and has had far-reaching effects on all areas of my life. I'm so at ease about the money, Carol. It's not a concern. I'm focusing my energy and my attention on things that really are going to matter in my life. That's been so critical in maintaining 'monetary sobriety,' as I call it. I abused money as I've abused alcohol in the past. My primary goal is to have a year's take-home salary in a savings account that is not used for anything other than if I'm unemployed. It's not money for vacations or a great deal on a new stereo system. No, it's money that sits there in the event that I'm unemployed.

"I was the cause of a minor car accident this summer that caused about a thousand dollars' worth of damage. I realized that if I went to my insurance company, my rates were almost guaranteed to double. So I looked at my little savings account and chose to pay for the repair out-of-pocket, promising myself to replace the money a little bit extra every week. I had a choice I've never had before because now I have an emergency savings account.

"Before, I felt a sense of hopelessness and a sense of shame. I felt I must be a bad person because I didn't manage my money well. I was constantly berating myself, 'Why can't I handle my money.' I was reliving all those messages I got when I was a child: 'You're just a kid, what would you know about money?' 'How much does that cost?' 'Well, that doesn't concern you, you're just a child.' There was a lot of fear, too, about what would happen if I couldn't pay my bills. What would happen if my parents found out that things weren't what they appeared to be? How would my friends react if they found out that I couldn't handle my money? And the way I responded to people who had money problems, 'Well, there must be something wrong with them' — as if it were some shameful secret.

"I'm a lot happier today than I was the day before I met you. I'm making progress. It's kind of rough at times, but I'm getting somewhere. I know I have these choices, these options. I'm in control of my life, and I don't feel like I'm stagnating. Emotionally and spiritually I'm far from stagnating. Getting control of my money made change possible."

There may be some surprises in store for us as our life with money comes under control. There were a few things for Anne that were a real switch from what she was used to. "For the first time in my life I'm having trouble with the IRS. I asked them, 'What do you mean I have to pay all this money on interest income?' Man, the IRS and me, boy did we get into it! I had to laugh because in the old days I never would have had this kind of stuff going on.

"I never thought I'd be paying a capital gains tax or tax on interest income. I thought 'Boy, you are really changing, you need someone to help you do your taxes.' It's so funny, all my life I only had to fill out one form, now I had to go get a whole bunch of them to explain all this stuff. So that's it, I said, and I got myself an accountant. I've become one of the bourgeoisie!"

As Connie changed her approach to money, her feelings about herself changed. "I never really took care of myself, my needs or my wants. Even though I'm very independent, active, and adventurous, still I was thinking, 'Well, if they happen, they happen.' I was getting a little burned out and maybe resentful of the hospital and nursing and work, work, work —

how boring. And I was beginning not to like myself. After taking the class, I said, 'Now wait a minute. I need the little things to look forward to. I work hard and I do a good job. I pay the bills, but there needs to be something to make me excited.'

"I had to change things within myself," said Connie, "and have something to look forward to. Now, I get all excited planning a trip, and I go to work and talk about it. I take the trip and then come back and share what happened. Before, I didn't take care of my goals and what I want that will make me happy. I'm a nurse, and I was taking care of everybody else but not really myself. It's funny how money fixed everything. I denied it before, absolutely denied it. But it's a real motivator and was very enlightening for me. I can't believe it. I *can* make things happen."

My friend the author Dan Jordan put it so well. "To know what you want and mean it takes guts. It takes courage to stick it out." One thing I know is that *you* have courage — I know it because you picked up this book about one of the most threatening subjects there is, money. Each time we courageously make the choice to act on what is best for us, we crank the quality of our lives up another notch. So use your courage to step right through your fears and apprehensions into action. Break through the walls that stop you. Go for it. This time you will succeed. Why? Because you've made the *choice* to succeed.

Our fears don't disappear overnight, and our money problems aren't solved in a day, but the steps we take pay big dividends from the very beginning. Amy wrote, "What I learned was that money could be a friend as well as a nightmare, depending on how I manage it. I pay myself first at least ten percent of my paycheck. I went with a credit union to avoid the bank blues, and I opened up different accounts for my various goals — especially an 'emergency' account. This has helped with big items such as license tags. I get paid a little better at my new job, but I still don't have $200 to spend freely at any one time.

"I take all my spare change and at the end of the day I put it in a jar. What goes in doesn't come out until the end of the month, when I roll it up and put it into one of my 'fun' accounts.

"Martial arts tournaments take me out of town, and it's so nice to have them paid off before I go! I'm probably not the best student, but I've made a few changes. As a friend of mine says, don't try to improve one thing 100%, just improve 100 things 1% and you've made a 100% improvement."

In our decision to act on something new we're turning the entire money mystique upside down. Everything's the same. Yet nothing's the same. We may *look* the same, but we sure don't *feel* the same. We're operating from a positive energy source that we were lacking before. We now have quality, fun, and a sense of purpose up front in our lives.

Lynn wrote, "Whoa! This is scary. I've been trying to save money, but I've never succeeded. Am I capable of it? I'm afraid if I try, I might never attain my goals, or if I do, they might not be what I wanted."

In the past we've played the "great escape." Unconsciously we know that we don't have to admit failure at something we haven't even tried. We fool ourselves by saying, "I've never wanted to travel or have the luxuries other people seem to want." The truth is, we're afraid to try, because if we try, we might fail, and how would we cope with another failure? This time you don't have to play that game, because this time you will succeed.

Others will notice the positive changes in you and will want to know your secret. Explaining your newfound enthusiasm may be tricky. It's difficult, because it's not the ¢hange in the jar or the diversified savings accounts that tell the story. The magic and the power are in the way you feel. By having a plan you have replaced hopelessness with hope. Depression and discouragement have been washed away by the joy and anticipation of dreams coming true. And the frightening and overwhelming feelings that once ruled have been replaced with the empowering feeling of being in control.

We're not just changing the way we handle our money, we're changing the way we handle our lives. We're experiencing the freedom of choice that comes with having money for what we love to do. We're more optimistic; we're happier. Is it any wonder people notice and want what we've found?

The next few months and years while you're building a base and becoming in control of your money are an excellent time to read and learn more about the ins and outs of the bigger world of money. I encourage you to attend free local financial seminars and check out money and investment books from the library. K.W. wrote, "I love reading books and articles, attending workshops, and listening to people talk about how to save money, live more economically, and simplify life. Your insight encouraged me to see through the media hype to decide for myself what is important in life."

Read, listen, and learn so that when your money foundation is solid and you are ready to "gamble" (invest), you will know something about investing. You'll be savvy and will either manage your own portfolio or will monitor the individuals and companies you put your trust and money in.

Investment clubs are an excellent way to begin learning about the stock market and to become an investor. Years ago ten of us got together and formed an investment club. We joined the National Association of Investors Corporation (NAIC) and received educational and support materials to get us started. We each contributed $10 a month that we pooled for buying stock. During the time between meetings each of us chose two stocks to research and chart. (The materials provided by NAIC taught us how.) For many of us the whole world of stock markets and investments is terribly intimidating. An investment club is a great way to learn firsthand about investing while in the supportive atmosphere of a group. To find an existing investment club near you or to learn how to start your own group, call or write the National Association of Investors Corporation, 1515 East 11 Mile Road, Royal Oak, Michigan 48067 (Tel. 313-543-0612).

My hope is that this book has been a grand invitation to you — an invitation to believe in yourself more fully, an invitation to bring that childlike energy inside you alive as you rekindle your hopes and dreams. My hope is that you have answered the invitation to unearth your deepest aspirations, promising to pay yourself first and pursue what has meaning for you. Old patterns of thinking and operating are resistant to change and very difficult to overcome. My hat is off to you as you purposefully carry out your plan for the quality of life you deserve.

Perhaps you have noticed my model of the even-paced tortoise appearing periodically throughout this book. The tortoise is significant for me because it reminds me of my father. My dad is my foremost model and inspiration for taking life at a steady, even pace. In addition, my father has instilled in me a spirited belief in myself. From time to time throughout my life, my dad has said, "Carol, if you are ever asked, 'Do you know how to do such-and-such?' be sure to answer, 'I've never done it before, but I know I'll be good at it.'"

My father's inspiring gift to me is now my gift to you. So I ask you, "Have you ever managed your money in such a way that you felt deeply satisfied and in control?" Now you answer boldly, "I've never done it before, but I know I'll be good at it!"

It has been an honor to share with you the ideas and stories in this book. Life is precious and you are precious. Listen to that wise and wonderful part of yourself that knows at every moment what is best for you and trust it. Remember that each time you choose a better quality of life for yourself, then you will have it to give to others. Be gentle with yourself. Old behaviors and patterns have deep roots. It will take time to establish a new way of operating, and it will take even longer for the new way to become more familiar than the old. Meanwhile, remind yourself to move along deliberately and contentedly like the tortoise, relishing the feeling of knowing you are moving closer and closer to the fulfillment of your dreams.

∾

You might be wondering, "Is Carol Keeffe getting what she wants in life?" My answer is, increasingly, yes. I am living and acting from my values more than ever and I'm getting better at it all the time. I love life and my greatest passion is spending time with people. In order to feel my best and be my best I dance (jitterbug), exercise regularly, eat a vegetarian diet (supporting the animal kingdom and helping to preserve the planet), and I've finally *acted* on my ten-year promise to keep myself relaxed by faithfully getting a weekly massage.

The more I claim what I really value in life, the more I savor precious moments. I celebrate you as you choose increasingly from what you value most. I wish you countless precious moments.

P.S. I'd *love* to hear from you.

✦ Please write and let me know what's been working for you. Who knows? Your story may help inspire someone else when it's used in future workshops or books.

✦ To place an order for the inexpensive Dream Box to help you play the ¢hange Game and make your dreams come true, just write or call.

✦ Let me know if you'd like me to custom-design a seminar or keynote speech for your group in either of my specialized areas: Money empowerment: *How to Get What You Want in Life with the Money You Already Have,* or increasing the quality of day-to-day life: *From Hassles to Harmony.*

✦ If you'd like to receive a list of our products or if you'd like to be added to our mailing list, just write:

Keeffe Seminars
P.O. Box 1965
Lynnwood, WA 98046
(206) 672-0212

On the next page is a list of affirmations. I encourage you to tear it out and post it where you'll read it aloud frequently. Each time you read these powerful statements, you'll feel a bit stronger and have a greater sense of purpose. Your ability to speak positively and with conviction about yourself and your approach to money management will help you move through the doubts and into the light of success in reaching your goals.

I Pay Myself First

I pay myself first each and every month.

I am important. I am setting money aside for my goals.

I am aware of more choices.

I spend only the money I have.

I pay only the *minimum* amount due on my installment bills.

I have written down my goals, and I am sticking to them.

I accept the challenge of making my money work for *me*.

I am in control of my money.

I am becoming financially *independent*.

I am *relaxed* knowing I have a plan for my income.

I am reaching my goals. My dreams are coming true.

The Garden Place

Ten percent of the profits from this book will go to help establish and maintain The Garden Place, a safe, supportive, and
life-giving retreat space for anyone desiring to further his or
her own personal growth.

Those who come to The Garden Place will benefit from
the profound personal growth and healing process called PRH
(Personnalité et Relations Humaines, or Personality and Human Relations). Founded by André Rochais and incorporated
in 1971, PRH makes available a wide variety of self-discovery
tools that can lead to greater fulfillment, happiness, and pro-
ductivity. PRH international headquarters is located at Poi-
tiers, France.

I was introduced to PRH educator Mary Ann O'Mara
(founder of The Garden Place) in 1986. Since that time the
personal growth tools I have acquired have helped me to
transform my life. If you are longing for deep inner happiness
on a regular basis and a stronger sense of purpose in your life,
PRH may be of interest to you.

Each year licensed PRH educators present more than two
thousand sessions in fifty-two countries. At this very moment,
more than thirty sessions are taking place around the world.

Thousands of men and women are discovering their best self, are improving their relationships, and are becoming more effectively involved in the welfare of society.

There are three legally incorporated PRH centers in the United States: Worcester, Massachusetts (508) 756-0978; Detroit, Michigan (313) 875-1125; and Marylhurst, Oregon (503) 635-9018; and one in Winnipeg, Manitoba, Canada (204) 237-4513.

For more information about The Garden Place, the PRH growth and healing process, or to make a donation, call (503) 635-9018 or write:

The Garden Place
PRH Institute, Inc.
Western Division
P.O. Box 127
Marylhurst, Oregon 97036

Index